Data Rookies Labs: Data Mining with R

Step-by-Step Mining Techniques

Data Analytics Curriculum, LLC

About the Publisher

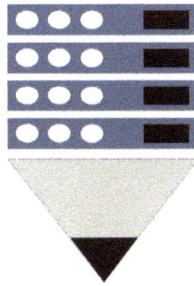

Data Analytics Curriculum

Data Analytics Curriculum, LLC creates approachable, visually engaging educational materials that make data science and technology accessible for learners from high school to college and independent study.

Please see our website or TPT online store for additional titles and resources such as slides, additional book forms, content (non lab) textbooks to accompany these labs, solution guides and other resources to help you teach and learn.

Additional resources available:

Website: https://www.dataanalyticscurriculum.com

Contents

Contents

Lab 1

Intro to R and RStudio

What is R and Why Use It?

R is a powerful and free programming language created specifically for statistical computing and data analysis. It has become popular across various fields such as data analytics, machine learning, and statistical analysis due to its extensive range of specialized packages tailored for data manipulation and interpretation. One of R's key strengths lies in its excellent data visualization capabilities, which allow users to create clear and insightful graphics. Additionally, it boasts strong libraries that support both statistical methods and machine learning techniques, making it a versatile tool for data professionals.

The language also benefits from a large and active community that contributes to its continuous improvement and offers support to users. Complementing R is RStudio, an Integrated Development Environment (IDE) that enhances the user experience by providing a more accessible interface, features like syntax highlighting, and various tools that help streamline the management of data projects, making it easier for both beginners and experienced users to work efficiently with R.

Part 1: Installing R and RStudio

Step 1: Download and Install R

Visit the R Project website: Go to https://www.r-project.org/

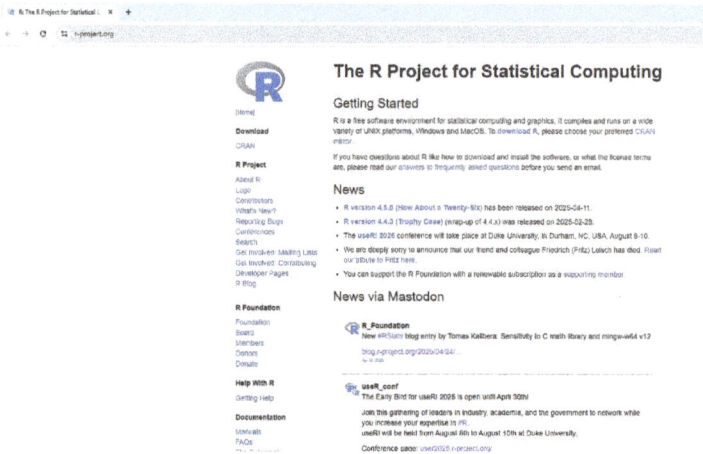

To install R, start by clicking on "CRAN" (Comprehensive R Archive Network) in the left sidebar of the website. Next, choose a mirror location that is close to you—any mirror in the USA works well for users in the United States. Then, select your operating system. For Windows, click on "Download R for Windows," then "base," and finally "Download R 4.x.x for Windows." Mac users should click on "Download R for macOS" and download the appropriate .pkg file for their system. If you are using Linux, follow the specific instructions provided for your distribution. Once the download is complete, run the installer and proceed with the default settings by clicking "Next" through the installation prompts.

Step 2: Download and Install RStudio

Note: You must install R first before installing RStudio, as RStudio requires R to function.

Visit RStudio's website: Go to https://posit.co/downloads/

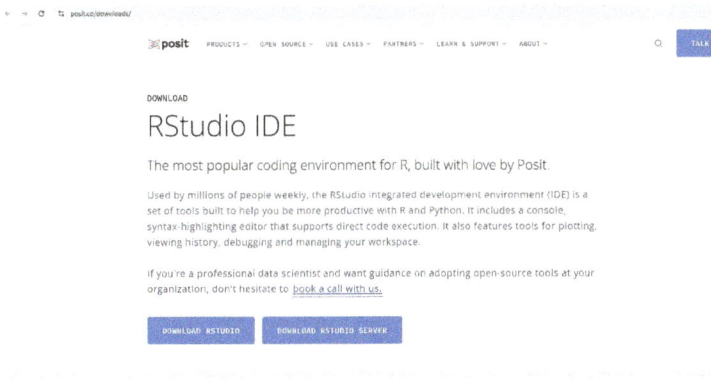

To install RStudio, scroll down the webpage until you find the section for RStudio Desktop, which is the free version. Click on "Download RStudio Desktop," then choose and download the installer that matches your operating system. Once the download is complete, run the installer and proceed with the default settings by simply clicking "Next" through the setup process.

Step 3: Verify Installation

Open RStudio (not R directly - we'll always use RStudio)

You should see a window with four panes (or three if it's your first time). In the bottom-left pane (Console), you should see something like:

If you see this, congratulations! You're ready to start using R.

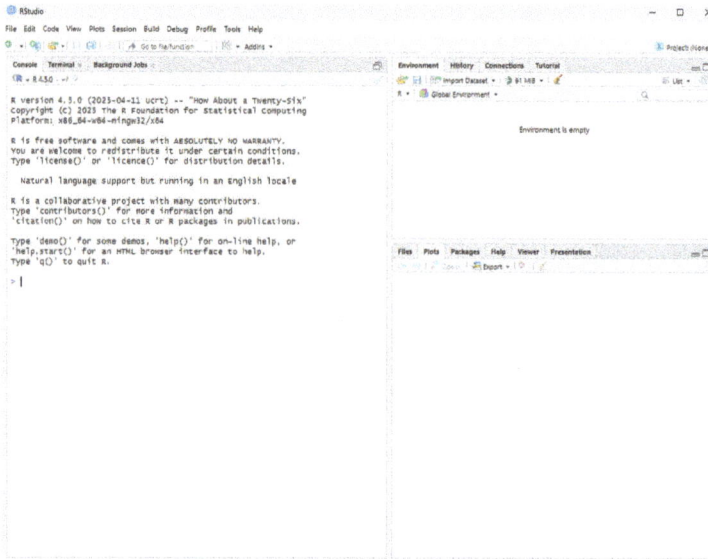

Part 2: The RStudio Interface

When you open RStudio, you'll see several panes. Initially there are three however go under file and do new R Script and the Script Editor appears.

Script Editor (Top-Left)

The Script Editor, located in the top-left panel of RStudio, is where you write and save your R scripts. It functions like a text editor specifically designed for writing R code, allowing you to organize and save your work for future use. From this panel, you can easily run individual lines or entire sections of code directly to the Console, making it a convenient space for developing and testing your code as you work through data analysis tasks.

Console (Bottom-Left)

The Console, found in the bottom-left panel of RStudio, is where R commands are executed. You can type commands directly into this space and see the results appear immediately below, making it useful for quick tests or interactive work. It's also where any code you run from the Script Editor will be processed, allowing you to view outputs, error messages, and other feedback in real time.

Environment/History (Top-Right)

The Environment/History panel, located in the top-right corner of RStudio, provides useful information about your current R session. The Environment tab displays all the data objects you've created, such as datasets, variables, and functions, allowing you to keep track of what's available in your workspace. The History tab keeps a record of all the commands you've run, making it easy to review, reuse, or modify previous code without having to retype it from memory.

Files/Plots/Packages/Help (Bottom-Right)

The Files/Plots/Packages/Help panel, located in the bottom-right corner of RStudio, serves several important functions. The Files tab lets you browse the files and folders on your computer, making it easy to locate and open your work. The Plots tab displays any graphs or visualizations you generate in R, allowing you to review and navigate through them. The Packages tab is where you can manage your R packages—these are add-on tools that extend R's capabilities, and you can install, load, or update them from this tab. Finally, the Help tab provides access to R's built-in documentation, offering detailed explanations and usage examples for functions and packages whenever you need guidance.

Part 3: Basic R Concepts

As a data analytics student, you'll primarily be running existing scripts rather than writing code from scratch. THIS IS NOT A PROGRAMMING COURSE OR BOOK. It is nice to have a programming background however the focus here is on USING and modifying existing scripts to perform data analytics tasks. You should be able to do this with a minimal programming background and should need to do little programming from scratch.

Working with Scripts

To open an existing R script in RStudio, go to the File menu, click on "Open File," and then select your .R file from your computer. Once your script is open, you can run your code in several ways. To execute a single line, place your cursor on that line and press Ctrl+Enter on Windows or Cmd+Enter on Mac. If you want to run multiple lines at once, highlight the lines you want to run and use the same keyboard shortcut. To run the entire script all at once, press Ctrl+Shift+Enter on Windows or Cmd+Shift+Enter on Mac. These shortcuts make it easy to test and execute your code efficiently.

Watch the output of running the script in the Console.

Understanding R Objects

In R, an object is simply a named piece of data that you create and store in your workspace. If you're new to programming, think of an object as a container that holds something—like a number, a list of names, a dataset, or even a graph. When you run code in R, you're often creating or modifying these objects. For example, if you type x <- 5, you're creating an object named x that stores the number 5. R has different types of objects depending on what kind of data you're working with. These include vectors (lists of values), data frames (tables of data), matrices (grids of numbers), and more. Understanding objects is important because everything you do in R—whether analyzing data, creating plots, or running models—usually involves creating and using these objects.

When you run scripts, you'll create different types of data objects. Primarily we will be creating or reading data frame objects either by typing in data or uploading a csv file for use in this book.

R Code

```
# Numbers

my_number <- 5

# Text (character strings)

my_text <- "Hello Data Mining"

# Vectors (lists of values)

my_numbers <- c(1, 2, 3, 4, 5)

my_names <- c("Alice", "Bob", "Charlie")

# Data frames (like Excel spreadsheets)

my_data <- data.frame(

name = c("Alice", "Bob", "Charlie"),

age = c(25, 30, 35),

score = c(85, 92, 78)
```

```
)
```

Reading Data Files

Most data analytics work starts with loading data in a preexisting file. These files can be read into R – the most easy way is to use csv files as these have no meta data or formatting (they are clean). Other files such as Excel require special packages to be loaded (see below on definition of a package). After data is loaded several functions allow you to view the data easily to validate the upload before using the data in analytics.

```
R Code
# Reading CSV files

data <- read.csv("mydata.csv")

# Reading Excel files (requires readxl package)

library(readxl)

data <- read_excel("mydata.xlsx")

# Viewing your data

View(data) # Opens data in a new tab

head(data) # Shows first 6 rows

summary(data) # Shows basic statistics
```

Part 4: R Packages

R packages are collections of functions, data, and documentation that extend the basic functionality of R, making it easier to perform specialized types of analysis. You can think of them as add-on toolkits designed for specific tasks, such as data visualization, machine learning, time series analysis, or text mining. Most R packages are open source and are created and shared by members of the global R community, including researchers, developers, and data professionals. These packages are typically hosted on CRAN (the Comprehensive R Archive Network), which is the official repository, but others may also be found on platforms like GitHub. Installing a package is simple: you can use the install.packages("package_name") command in the Console, or you can go to the Packages tab in RStudio and use the interface to search for and install packages. Once installed, packages need to be loaded into your session using the library(package_name) function before you can use their tools.

Installing Packages

You only need to install a package once (downloading it form online source) and then it will live on your local machine (unless you delete the files where it is stored or otherwise alter things).

```
R Code
# Install a single packageinstall.packages("ggplot2")


# Install multiple packagesinstall.packages(c("dplyr", "tidyr",
"caret"))
```

Loading Packages

You need to load packages every time you start RStudio so that they are available in the current working project environment.

```
R Code
# Load a packagelibrary(ggplot2)

# Or multiple packages

library(dplyr)

library(tidyr)

library(caret)
```

Essential Packages for data analytics

Here are some packages often used in data analytics (some of which we will use in labs in coming chapters).

- **dplyr**: Data manipulation (filtering, sorting, summarizing)

- **ggplot2**: Creating beautiful visualizations

- **caret**: Machine learning and classification

- **randomForest**: Random forest algorithms

- **e1071**: Support vector machines and other ML algorithms

- **cluster**: Clustering analysis

- **arules**: Association rule mining

• **rpart**: Decision trees

Part 5: Common Script Patterns

When working with R scripts, you typically start by loading your dataset—for example, from a CSV file—and then perform a quick exploration to understand its size, column names, structure, and summary statistics. In R, many operations you perform are done using functions, which are like little machines or tools that take some input, process it, and give you an output. For example, read.csv() is a function that reads data from a CSV file and loads it into R. Functions always have a name followed by parentheses, where you put any information they need, called arguments. Here's how you might load data and explore it:

```
R Code
# Load data

data <- read.csv("sales_data.csv")

# Quick exploration

dim(data) # Dimensions (rows, columns)

names(data) # Column names

str(data) # Structure of data

summary(data) # Summary statistics
```

When working with data frames (tables), you can use the $ operator to access specific columns by name. For example, data$price refers to the "price" column inside the dataset, letting you analyze or plot that specific variable.

In R, functions are individual commands or tools that perform specific tasks, such as calculating a mean or creating a plot. On the other hand, packages are collections of related functions and datasets bundled together to extend R's capabilities. Think of packages as toolkits or libraries that you install and load when you want extra features beyond base R. For example, the ggplot2 package contains many functions specifically designed for advanced data visualization.

After loading and exploring data, you often use functions to create simple visualizations or calculate basic statistics. For example, plot() creates a scatterplot, hist() creates a histogram, and mean() calculates the average value of a variable. Here are some examples:

```
# Create simple plots

# Scatter plot of price vs. quantity
plot(data$price, data$quantity)

hist(data$price) # Histogram of price

# Basic statistics

mean(data$price) # Mean price

median(data$price) # Median price

table(data$category) # Frequency count of categories
```

Part 6: Tips for Success

Set Your Working Directory

In R, the working directory is the folder on your computer where R looks for files to read and where it saves files by default. It's important to set your working directory to the location where your data files are stored so that you can easily load and save files without typing long file paths. You can set the working directory in R using the setwd() function with the path to your folder, for example:

```
R Code
setwd("C:/Users/YourName/Documents/DataMining").
```

Alternatively, if you're using RStudio, you can set it through the menu by going to the menu bar and Session → Set Working Directory → Choose Directory and selecting the appropriate folder. Setting your working directory correctly helps keep your projects organized and makes working with data files smoother.

File Management

When working in R, it's important to regularly save your progress to avoid losing any of your code or data. The scripts you write in R, which contain your R code, can be saved by pressing Ctrl+S on Windows or Cmd+S on a Mac. These script files usually have the extension .R. Saving your script means your code is safely stored on your computer and can be opened, edited, or run again later without starting from scratch.

Beyond saving scripts, R has something called a workspace, which you can think of as the current memory of your R session. The workspace holds all the data objects, variables, and functions you have created during your work.

Saving the workspace means saving everything you've done so far so that when you come back later, you don't have to reload or recreate all your data and settings — you can pick up exactly where you left off.

To keep everything related to a specific analysis or project organized, RStudio offers a helpful feature called Projects. A project bundles together all your scripts, data files, workspace, and any other documents into a single folder. This way, when you open a project, all the files and information you need for that particular task are in one place. This organization is especially useful if you are working on multiple assignments or analyses at the same time because it prevents files from getting mixed up or lost.

You can create a new project easily in RStudio by going to File → New Project. Using projects helps make your workflow smoother and your work more manageable. So, in summary, regularly save your .R scripts to keep your code safe, save your workspace to keep your data and variables intact, and use RStudio projects to keep everything related to your work well-organized.

Getting Help

When you're working in R, it's common to need help understanding what a function does or how to use it. A strength of R is the well written internal help support system. One way to get help is by typing commands directly in the Console. For example, if you want to learn about the mean() function, you can type ?mean and press Enter, and R will show the documentation for that function. Similarly, if you want to search for help on a topic or keyword, like "clustering," you can type ??clustering to find all related help pages.

In addition to these commands, RStudio provides a very useful Help pane located in the bottom-right corner of the interface. This Help pane allows you to search for functions, packages, and topics without needing to remember the exact commands. You can simply type a keyword or function name into the search box, and relevant help files and guides will appear for you to browse. Clicking on any of these entries will open detailed documentation, including examples of how to use the function, explanations of its arguments, and additional resources.

Using both the help commands (? and ??) in the Console and the Help pane in RStudio gives you quick and easy access to the information you need, making it much easier to learn and troubleshoot as you work with R.

Common Errors and Solutions

As you run script in R the Console will have error messages. Get familiar with what these mean in case you need to trouble shoot.

Error: "Object not found"

- Solution: Make sure you've run the code that creates the object

- Check spelling and capitalization (R is case-sensitive)

Error: "Package not found"

- Solution: Install the package first with install.packages("packagename")

Error: "Cannot find file"

- Solution: Check your working directory and file path

- Use getwd() to see current directory

Best Practices for Script Users

When working with scripts, start by reading the comments—these are lines beginning with # that often explain what each part of the code does. Avoid running the entire script all at once right away; instead, run it section by section to better understand how it works and catch errors early. As you go, check the Environment pane to confirm that variables and objects are being created as expected. Keep your data files well-organized by placing them in the same folder as your scripts, which helps avoid file path issues. Finally, always make a backup copy of the original script before making any changes, so you can easily revert if needed.

Lab 2

Exploring Data

Introduction

Exploring data is a critical first step in any data analysis project. Before data mining analysts must understand the structure, distribution, and relationships within the data.

In this lab, you'll learn how to create and inspect a dataset, confirm and clean data types, summarize key statistics, visualize distributions and relationships, and save your outputs for reuse.

Lesson Steps

Step 1: Start a New R Script

Open RStudio and start a new script (File > New File > R Script). Save this script to your working folder with a name like `el_nino_analysis.R`. Use `setwd()` or the menu (under Session) if you need to change the working directory (note the slash direction in file paths in R is not the same as Windows). Your working directory can be anywhere (although a location on the local machine is best) and is where your workspace where all steps in the tutorial will be documented and saved.

Step 2: Load Required Packages

This tutorial uses the tidyverse collection of packages, which includes tools for reading data, transforming it, and creating visualizations. Load the package using the following code. If you haven't installed it yet, you'll need to install it first using `install.packages("tidyverse")`. The logic code here tests whether the package has already been installed (downloaded for local use) or not before loading it into the active R session.

```
R Code
# Install if not already installed
options(repos = c(CRAN = "https://cran.r-project.org"))


install.packages("tidyverse")


# Load package
library(tidyverse)
```

Step 3: Create the Dataset

Instead of loading data we'll directly create the dataset el_nino in R. This dataset includes the year, El Niño classification, number of storms, and number of hurricanes.

R Code

```
# Create el_nino dataset
el_nino <- data.frame(
  year = 1950:1997,
  el.nino = c(
    "cold", "warm", "neutral", "warm",
    "cold", "cold", "neutral", "warm",
    "neutral", "neutral", "neutral",
    "cold", "neutral", "neutral", "cold",
    "warm", "neutral", "cold", "neutral",
    "neutral", "cold", "cold", "warm",
    "cold", "cold", "cold", "warm", "warm",
    "neutral", "neutral", "neutral",
    "neutral", "warm", "warm", "neutral",
    "cold", "warm", "warm", "cold",
    "cold", "neutral", "warm", "warm",
    "warm", "warm", "cold", "cold", "warm"
  ),
  storms = c(
    13, 10, 7, 14, 11, 12, 8, 8, 10, 11, 7,
    11, 5, 9, 12, 6, 11, 8, 7, 17, 10,
    13, 4, 7, 7, 8, 8, 6, 11, 8, 11, 11,
    5, 4, 12, 11, 6, 7, 12, 11, 14, 8, 6,
    8, 7, 19, 13, 7
  ),
  hurricanes = c(
    11, 8, 6, 6, 8, 9, 4, 3, 7, 7, 4,
    8, 3, 7, 6, 4, 7, 6, 4, 12, 5, 6, 3,
    4, 4, 6, 6, 5, 5, 5, 9, 7, 2, 3, 5,
    7, 4, 3, 5, 7, 8, 4, 3, 4, 3, 11,
    9, 3
```

```
   )
)


# Preview the structure
el_nino[1:4,]
```

Output

```
##   year el.nino storms hurricanes
## 1 1950    cold     13         11
## 2 1951    warm     10          8
## 3 1952 neutral      7          6
## 4 1953    warm     14          6
```

Step 4: Check and Set Column Data Types

Although R often infers column types correctly when creating a data frame, it's good practice to confirm or explicitly set them. We'll make sure the year and hurricanes columns are integers, storms is numeric (double), and el.nino is character.

```
R Code
# Load dplyr if needed
library(dplyr)

# Ensure correct data types
el_nino <- el_nino %>%
  mutate(
    year = as.integer(year),
    el.nino = as.character(el.nino),
    storms = as.numeric(storms),
    hurricanes = as.integer(hurricanes)
  )

# Preview the structure
el_nino[1:4,]
```

```
Output
##    year el.nino storms  hurricanes
## 1 1950    cold      13          11
## 2 1951    warm      10           8
## 3 1952 neutral       7           6
## 4 1953    warm      14           6
```

This guarantees that your data types are exactly what you expect before continuing with any analysis.

Step 5: Explore Basic Statistics

Exploring new data with basic statistics is important to look at. The `summary()` function in R provides a quick overview of the key statistics for all variables. This includes measures like mean, median, min, and max for numeric data, and counts for categorical data.

R Code
```
# Basic statistics with summary
summary(el_nino[,1:2])
```

Output
```
##       year          el.nino
##   Min.   :1950   Length:48
##   1st Qu.:1962   Class :character
##   Median :1974   Mode  :character
##   Mean   :1974
##   3rd Qu.:1985
##   Max.   :1997
```

R Code
```
summary(el_nino[,3:4])
```

Output

```
##       storms         hurricanes
##   Min.   : 4.000   Min.   : 2.00
##   1st Qu.: 7.000   1st Qu.: 4.00
##   Median : 8.500   Median : 5.50
##   Mean   : 9.396   Mean   : 5.75
##   3rd Qu.:11.000   3rd Qu.: 7.00
##   Max.   :19.000   Max.   :12.00
```

Step 6: Visualize Distributions with Histograms

Histograms are useful for understanding the shape of numeric data. Often, looking for how normally distributed that data is important to evaluate if data meet this for an analytical assumption. Let's look at a histogram of the `storms` numeric variable.

R Code

```
# Histogram
ggplot(el_nino, aes(x = storms)) +
  geom_histogram(binwidth = 0.5, fill = "#637D8D") +
  theme_minimal() +
  labs(title = "Distribution of Storms")
```

Distribution of Storms

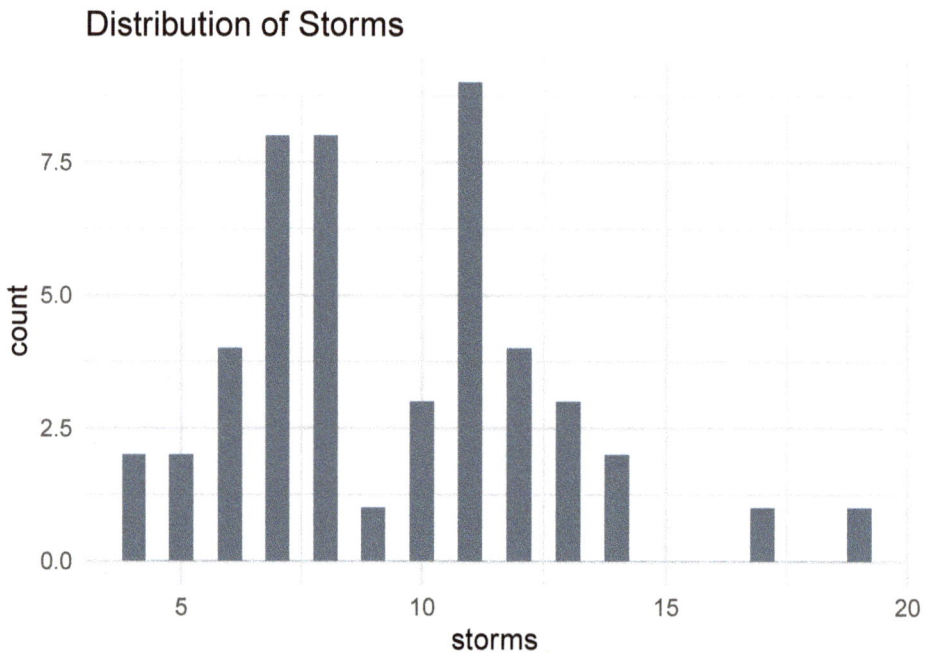

The resulting histogram is displayed below.

Step 7: Create Box Plots

Box plots summarize the distribution of a numeric variable and show medians and outliers. You can create a box plot to compare number of storms by El Niño category.

```
R Code
# Boxplot
ggplot(el_nino, aes(x = el.nino, y = storms)) +
  geom_boxplot(fill = "#3D5A80") +
  theme_minimal() +
  labs(title = "Storms by El Niño Category",
       x = "El Niño Category", y = "Number of Storms")
```

Storms by El Niño Category

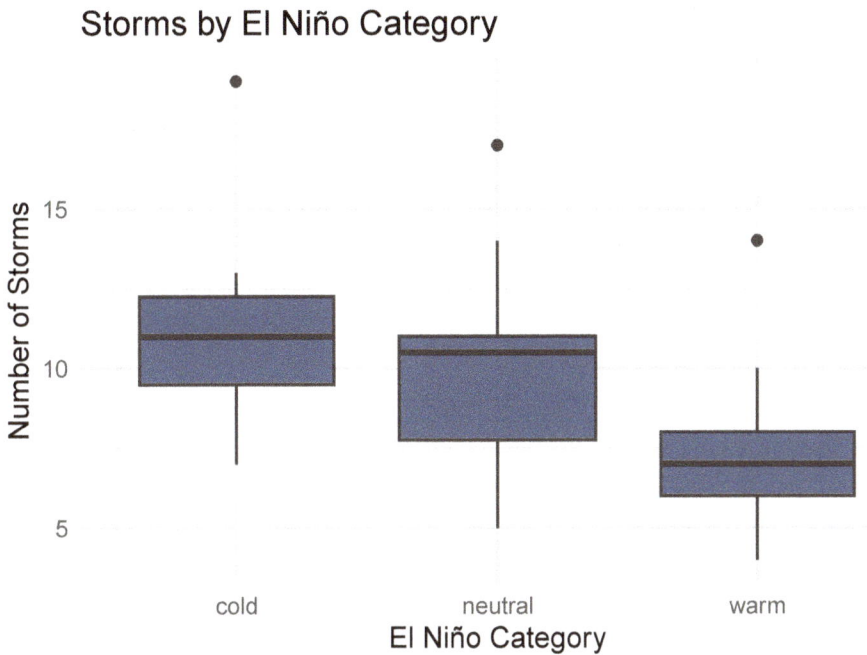

The box plot produced helps understand the relation of El Niño and storms.

Step 8: Create Scatter Plots

Scatter plots help explore relationships between two numeric variables. Here, you will plot the number of hurricanes against number of storms to check for any visible trends or correlations.

```
R Code
# Scatterplot
ggplot(el_nino, aes(x = storms, y = hurricanes)) +
  geom_point(color = "#EE6C4D") +
  theme_minimal() +
  labs(
    title = "Hurricanes vs. Storms",
    x = "Number of Storms",
    y = "Number of Hurricanes"
  )
```

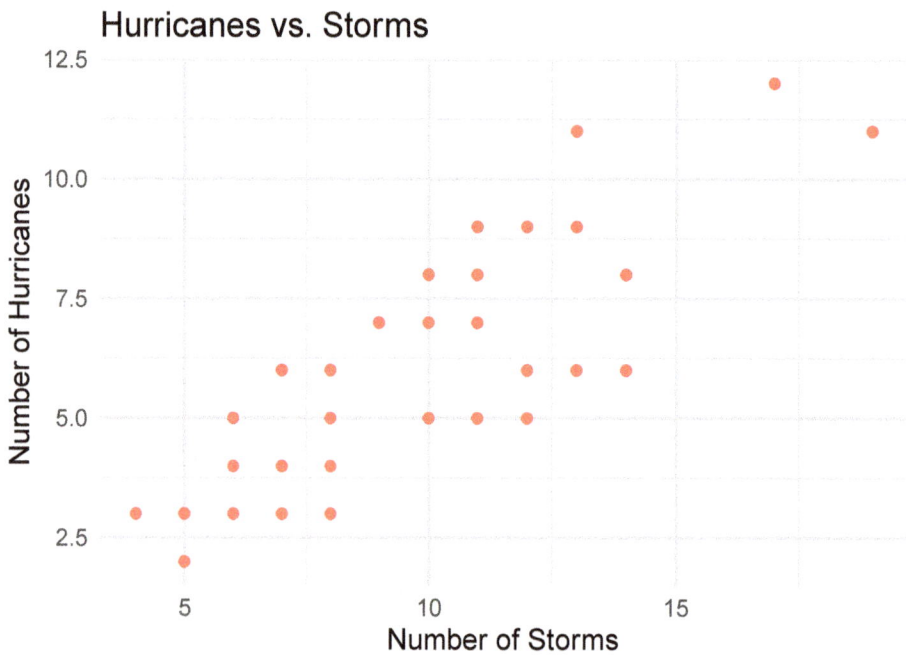

Hurricanes vs. Storms

The scatterplot clarifies the positively correlated linear relation between storms and hurricanes.

Step 9: Save Data and Plots

Saving your work allows you to reuse and share it. Plots made using the `ggplot` package may be exported to your working directory using function `ggsave()`. Note this function is only for `ggplot` produced plots (it does not work with base R plots).

```
R Code
# Write csv
write_csv(el_nino, "processed_elNino.csv")


# Save plot
ggsave("hurricanes_vs_storms.png")
```

Wrap-Up

In this lab, you created and structured a dataset in R, verified and cleaned data types, explored basic statistics and summaries, created insightful visualizations, and saved your outputs for future use. These are foundational data skills that you'll rely on throughout your data analysis work.

Exercises

Exploring Data

Exploratory data analysis is an essential first step to understanding any dataset. These exercises practice creating datasets, inspecting data structure, summarizing key statistics, and visualizing distributions and relationships using R.

Dataset 1: Plant Growth Measurements

```
R Code
plant_growth <- data.frame(
  PlantID = paste0("P", 1:10),
  Height_cm = c(
    23.4, 25.1, 22.8, 24.7, 26.3, 21.9,
    23.5, 24.0, 25.7, 22.3
  ),
  Leaf_Count = c(
    15, 17, 14, 16, 18, 13, 15,
    16, 17, 14
  ),
  Flower_Count = c(5, 7, 6, 8, 9, 4, 5, 7, 8, 6),
  Water_ml = c(
    500, 520, 480, 510, 530, 470, 495,
    505, 525, 485
  )
)
```

1. Print the `plant_growth` data frame to view all observations and variables.

2. Use `str()` or `glimpse()` to check the data structure and data types.

3. Calculate summary statistics (mean, median, min, max) for `Height_cm` and `Leaf_Count`.

4. Create a histogram of `Height_cm` to observe the distribution of plant heights.

5. Plot a scatter plot of `Water_ml` vs `Flower_Count` and describe any apparent relationship.

Dataset 2: Car Specifications

```
R Code
car_specs <- data.frame(
  Model = c(
    "Sedan1", "SUV1", "Coupe1", "Sedan2",
    "SUV2", "Coupe2", "Sedan3", "SUV3"
  ),
  Horsepower = c(
    150, 200, 180, 160, 210, 175,
    155, 205
  ),
  Weight_kg = c(
    1200, 1600, 1300, 1250, 1650,
    1280, 1220, 1620
  ),
  MPG = c(30, 22, 28, 31, 20, 27, 29, 21)
)
```

6. Display the `car_specs` data frame.

7. Check the data types of all columns and ensure `Horsepower` and

Weight_kg are numeric.

8. Find the mean and standard deviation of MPG (miles per gallon).

9. Generate a box plot comparing MPG across the different car models.

10. Create a scatter plot of Horsepower vs Weight_kg and interpret the trend.

Dataset 3: Student Test Scores

```
R Code
student_scores <- data.frame(
  StudentID = paste0("S", 1:12),
  Math = c(
    78, 85, 92, 88, 74, 80, 90, 95,
    83, 87, 91, 76
  ),
  English = c(
    82, 79, 88, 90, 75, 85, 87, 93,
    80, 86, 89, 78
  ),
  Science = c(
    85, 88, 90, 92, 78, 84, 89, 94,
    82, 90, 91, 79
  )
)
```

11. View the entire student_scores data frame.

12. Check the summary statistics for the Math and Science scores.

13. Create a histogram for the English scores to check for distribution

shape.

14. Plot a scatter plot comparing `Math` and `Science` scores to examine their relationship.

15. Identify any students who scored above 90 in both `Math` and `Science`.

Lab 3

Normalizing Data with Z-Scores

Introduction

In data mining an issue that often arises is that the data is on various measurement scales. For example length may be measured in inches or centimeters. The scale of these is different (the same thing the measures 1 inch measures 2.54 cm and so something measured in cm appears in units larger than in inches and the two unit scales are not directly comparable) and causes problems in data mining. Therefore before doing much work in data mining we usually rescale quantitative data to a standardized scale.

This lab will guide you through one of the simplest and most common methods of normalization—Z-score normalization, also known as standardization (this is in fact the standard normal distribution that will be used). You will learn what Z-scores are, why they are useful, and how to calculate them.

Z-score normalization transforms numeric data so that each value represents how far it is from the mean, measured in standard deviations. After this transformation, the variable will have a mean of 0 and a standard deviation of 1. This allows values to be compared even if they originally came from variables with very different scales.

The formula for computing the Z-score of a value is:

$$z = \frac{x - \mu}{\sigma}$$

In this equation: x is the original value, μ is the mean of the variable, σ is the standard deviation.

The resulting value, z, tells us how many standard deviations the original value is above or below the mean.

Lesson Steps

Step 1: Creating a Sample Dataset

To begin, we will create a small dataset in R. This dataset contains information for eight students, including how many hours they studied, their test scores, and how many hours they slept. All 3 of these are on different measurement scales - because test scores is the largest values if we did analysis using this in many data miing techniques this variable would dominate or be the most influential because of this - we don't want this which is the purpose of resetting the data to normalized values instead.

R Code

```
# Create example dataset
data <- data.frame(
  Student_ID = 1:8,
  Hours_Studied = c(2, 4, 6, 8, 10, 12, 14, 16),
  Test_Score = c(55, 60, 65, 70, 75, 80, 85, 90),
  Sleep_Hours = c(8, 7.5, 7, 6.5, 6, 5.5, 5, 4.5)
)


# Print dataset
print(data)
```

Output

```
##    Student_ID Hours_Studied Test_Score Sleep_Hours
## 1           1             2         55         8.0
## 2           2             4         60         7.5
## 3           3             6         65         7.0
## 4           4             8         70         6.5
## 5           5            10         75         6.0
## 6           6            12         80         5.5
## 7           7            14         85         5.0
## 8           8            16         90         4.5
```

Step 2: Manually Calculating the Z-Score for One Column

We start by standardizing just one of the variables—Hours_Studied. First, calculate the mean and standard deviation. Then apply the Z-score formula and store the results in a new column.

```
R Code
# Manual computation of z-scores
mean_hours <- mean(data$Hours_Studied)
sd_hours <- sd(data$Hours_Studied)


# Create a new column with standardized scores
numerator<-data$Hours_Studied - mean_hours
data$Hours_Studied_Z <- numerator / sd_hours


# View results
data[,1:3]
```

```
Output
##    Student_ID Hours_Studied Test_Score
## 1           1             2         55
## 2           2             4         60
## 3           3             6         65
## 4           4             8         70
## 5           5            10         75
## 6           6            12         80
## 7           7            14         85
## 8           8            16         90
```

```
R Code
data[,4:5]
```

```
Output
##    Sleep_Hours Hours_Studied_Z
## 1          8.0      -1.4288690
## 2          7.5      -1.0206207
## 3          7.0      -0.6123724
## 4          6.5      -0.2041241
## 5          6.0       0.2041241
## 6          5.5       0.6123724
## 7          5.0       1.0206207
## 8          4.5       1.4288690
```

Step 3: Creating a Z-Score Function

To standardize multiple columns more efficiently, we define a function to compute Z-scores and then apply it to the other numeric variables.

```
R Code
# Z-score function
z_score <- function(x) {
  (x - mean(x)) / sd(x)
}


# Apply function to other variables
data$Test_Score_Z <- z_score(data$Test_Score)
data$Sleep_Hours_Z <- z_score(data$Sleep_Hours)


# View updated dataset
data[,1:4]
```

Output

```
##   Student_ID Hours_Studied Test_Score Sleep_Hours
## 1          1             2         55         8.0
## 2          2             4         60         7.5
## 3          3             6         65         7.0
## 4          4             8         70         6.5
## 5          5            10         75         6.0
## 6          6            12         80         5.5
## 7          7            14         85         5.0
## 8          8            16         90         4.5
```

R Code

```
data[,5:7]
```

Output

```
##   Hours_Studied_Z Test_Score_Z Sleep_Hours_Z
## 1      -1.4288690   -1.4288690     1.4288690
## 2      -1.0206207   -1.0206207     1.0206207
## 3      -0.6123724   -0.6123724     0.6123724
## 4      -0.2041241   -0.2041241     0.2041241
## 5       0.2041241    0.2041241    -0.2041241
## 6       0.6123724    0.6123724    -0.6123724
## 7       1.0206207    1.0206207    -1.0206207
## 8       1.4288690    1.4288690    -1.4288690
```

Step 4: Understanding the Results

If data is not standardized, variables with larger scales—such as income measured in thousands—can overpower variables with smaller scales—like satisfaction ratings from 1 to 5. This can distort distance calculations and affect how variance is interpreted in the analysis.

By applying Z-score scaling, each variable contributes equally to the analysis in terms of variance. For example, if you have one variable ranging from 0 to 100 and another from 0 to 10, standardization will adjust both so that their values are centered at zero and have a consistent spread. This makes their influence in the analysis more balanced.

Wrap-Up

Z-score normalization, also known as standardization, transforms each variable so that it has a mean of zero and a standard deviation of one. This step is important when using methods like clustering, principal component analysis (PCA) and many data mining algorithms that are sensitive to the scale of the data.

Exercises

Normalizing Data

In this exercise set, you will practice Z-score normalization.

Weather Data

```
R Code
weather_data <- data.frame(
  Day = 1:8,
  Temperature = c(72, 75, 78, 74, 76, 77, 79, 73),
  Wind_Speed = c(5, 7, 6, 5, 8, 7, 6, 5),
  Humidity = c(55, 50, 60, 52, 58, 53, 59, 51)
)
```

1. Print the data frame and show R output.

2. Calculate the mean and standard deviation for the Temperature column. Show your R code and output.

3. Manually compute the Z-scores for the Temperature column using the formula. Show your code.

4. Show the new data frame with the new column with standard scores for temperature.

5. Write a function to compute z scores. Use this function to compute standard scores for humidity and windspeed and store these in two new variables in the data frame. Show your R code.

6. Show your data frame with all variables standardized.

Web Session Data

```
R Code
web_data <- data.frame(
  Session = 1:8,
  Time_on_Site = c(5.2, 4.8, 6.1, 5.5, 7.0, 3.8,
                   4.5, 6.5),
  Pages_Viewed = c(8, 6, 10, 9, 12, 5, 7, 11)
)
```

7. Print the data frame and show R output.

8. Use the same function written for the weather data to compute standard scores for time on site and pages viewed. Store the new variables in the data frame. Show your R code.

9. Show your data frame with all variables standardized.

10. Why is it important to use Z-score normalization?

Lab 4

Principal Component Analysis (PCA)

Introduction

In many real-world datasets, especially those involving measurements of related variables, the data can be complex and have a lot of features (aka variables). In addition many variables may be highly correlated, making it difficult to analyze and visualize.

Principal Component Analysis (PCA) is a statistical technique that helps simplify such data by reducing its dimensionality while preserving as much variability as possible. By transforming the original correlated variables into a smaller set of uncorrelated variables called principal components, PCA reveals the underlying patterns and structure in the data. This lab demonstrates how to perform PCA on a simulated dataset of chemical properties, guiding you through data preparation, analysis, interpretation of results, and visualization. The goal is to gain insight into how PCA can summarize complex multivariate data effectively.

Lesson Steps

Step 1: Create a Simulated Dataset

First, we create a dataset with 10 samples and 4 numeric variables representing chemical properties such as acidity, sugar content, aroma, and bitterness. These measurements are on different scales.

```
R Code
set.seed(123)
food_data <- data.frame(
  Sample = paste0("S", 1:10),
  Acidity = round(rnorm(10, mean = 5.2, sd = 0.5), 2),
  Sugar = round(rnorm(10, mean = 12.5, sd = 1.2), 2),
  Aroma = round(rnorm(10, mean = 7.5, sd = 0.8), 2),
  Bitterness = round(rnorm(10, mean = 4.5, sd = 0.4), 2)
)
```

Step 2: Select Numeric Features for PCA

PCA requires numeric input, so we exclude the sample identifier and select only the chemical property columns.

```
R Code
features <- food_data[, c("Acidity", "Sugar",
                          "Aroma", "Bitterness")]
```

By focusing on numeric variables, we ensure PCA analyzes meaningful quantitative differences among samples.

Step 3: Standardize the Data

Because the variables have different units and scales, we standardize each variable to have a mean of zero and standard deviation of one using z-score normalization.

R Code

```
features_scaled <- scale(features)


features_scaled
```

Output

```
##             Acidity        Sugar      Aroma Bitterness
##   [1,] -0.667057844  0.98032014 -0.6873064  0.1898791
##   [2,] -0.331431256  0.14532182  0.2273088 -1.1867445
##   [3,]  1.556468303  0.18546597 -0.6469558  1.0918050
##   [4,]  0.004195332 -0.09554308 -0.3241504  1.0443352
##   [5,]  0.046148656 -0.73784947 -0.2165486  0.9493956
##   [6,]  1.724281597  1.51825174 -1.3598176  0.7120467
##   [7,]  0.402751906  0.28181193  1.3571276  0.4272280
##   [8,] -1.401241006 -2.09472173  0.6173653 -0.7120467
##   [9,] -0.792917815  0.47450385 -0.7680078 -1.1867445
## [10,] -0.541197873 -0.65756117  1.8009850 -1.3291539
## attr(,"scaled:center")
##    Acidity      Sugar      Aroma Bitterness
##      5.238     12.749      7.161      4.630
## attr(,"scaled:scale")
##    Acidity      Sugar      Aroma Bitterness
##  0.4767203  1.2455115  0.7434820  0.2106603
```

Step 4: Perform PCA

With the standardized data, we run PCA using the `prcomp()` function without additional centering or scaling (since already done).

```
R Code
pca_result <- prcomp(features_scaled,
            center = FALSE, scale. = FALSE)
pca_result
```

```
Output
## Standard deviations (1, .., p=4):
## [1] 1.5726133 0.8929080 0.7370758 0.4316503
##
## Rotation (n x k) = (4 x 4):
##                    PC1         PC2         PC3         PC4
## Acidity      0.5452908  -0.3000968  -0.4695369   0.6262068
## Sugar        0.4871204   0.5716077  -0.4473363  -0.4856631
## Aroma       -0.4820725  -0.4081374  -0.7110389  -0.3089555
## Bitterness   0.4826777  -0.6454691   0.2717516  -0.5258735
```

After running Principal Component Analysis (PCA) on the standardized data, R provides two important pieces of output. The first is a list of standard deviations for each of the new principal components, and the second is a matrix of loadings, which shows how much each original variable contributes to the components.

The standard deviations of the four principal components are as follows: the first component (PC1) has a standard deviation of approximately 1.57, the second component (PC2) has a standard deviation of about 0.89, the third (PC3) is around 0.74, and the fourth (PC4) is about 0.43. Since the standard deviation reflects how much variance each component captures, we can use these values to understand which components are most important. Larger standard deviations indicate that the component explains more of the original data's variability. In this case, PC1 explains the most variation by far, followed by PC2, PC3, and then PC4.

To better understand what each component represents, we examine the rotation matrix, also known as the loadings matrix. These values show the contribution of each original variable—Acidity, Sugar, Aroma, and Bitterness—to each principal component. For PC1, Acidity has a loading of 0.55, Sugar is 0.49, Bitterness is 0.48, and Aroma has a negative loading of -0.48. This pattern suggests that PC1 measures overall flavor strength, where higher Acidity, Sugar, and Bitterness increase the PC1 score, while higher Aroma reduces it. In other words, a sample with a high PC1 score would have strong flavors in all areas except Aroma, which would be relatively weaker. Because this component captures the largest share of the variation in the data, we can consider it the most meaningful summary of the dataset.

For PC2, the loadings tell a different story. Sugar contributes positively with a loading of 0.57, while Bitterness has a strong negative loading of -0.65. Acidity and Aroma both have smaller negative contributions. This shows that PC2 mostly reflects a contrast between sweet and bitter characteristics. A sample that scores high on PC2 is likely to be sweeter and less bitter, whereas a low PC2 score would represent a sample that is more bitter and less sweet. This component explains a smaller but still significant portion of the data variation.

PC3 is shaped most strongly by Aroma, which has a large negative loading of -0.71. This means PC3 primarily captures differences in Aroma, and to a lesser extent, other small contrasts in the other variables. Bitterness slightly contributes positively here, with a loading of about 0.27. Because this component explains even less variance than PC2, it may reflect finer or more subtle differences in the flavor profile.

PC4 contributes the least to the overall variation in the data. Its largest loading is from Acidity, with a value of about 0.63. However, because this component explains only a small proportion of the total variance (about 4%), it may be picking up leftover noise or very specific variation that isn't broadly useful for summarizing the dataset.

In summary, the results from this step of PCA show us that most of the important information in the dataset can be captured using just the first two principal components. PC1, which reflects overall flavor intensity with higher values for Acidity, Sugar, and Bitterness and lower values for Aroma, accounts for the majority of the variation. PC2, which contrasts sweetness and bitterness, explains another significant portion. The other components add smaller, less impactful details. Together, these findings help us reduce the complexity of the dataset while keeping the key patterns intact.

Step 5: Evaluate Explained Variance with Scree Plot

We calculate the proportion of total variance explained by each PC and visualize this with a scree plot.

```
R Code
explained_var <- pca_result$sdev^2 / sum(pca_result$sdev^2)
plot(explained_var, type = "b", xlab = "Principal Component",
     ylab = "Proportion of Variance Explained",
     main = "Scree Plot")
```

Scree Plot

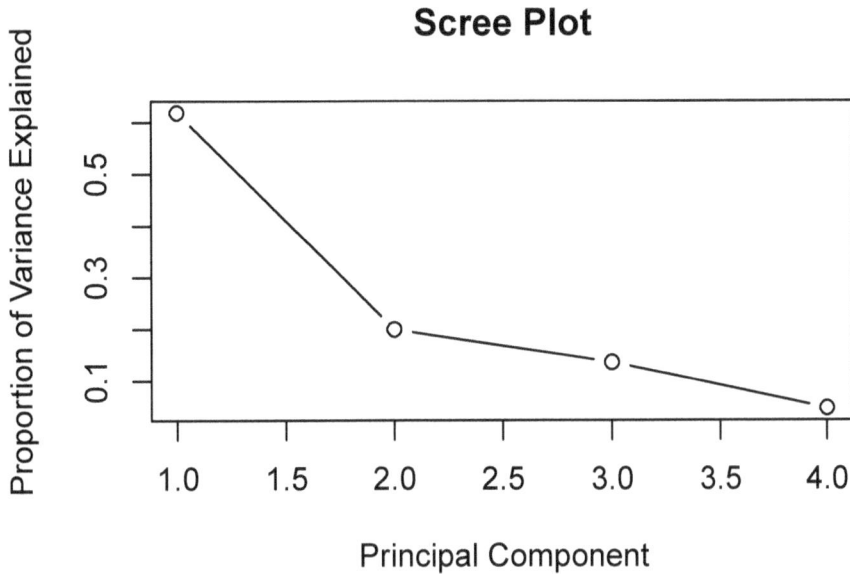

The scree plot shows how much variation each PC accounts for. Typically, the first PC explains the most variance, with subsequent PCs explaining less. We look for an "elbow" point where additional PCs add little explanatory power. Choosing enough PCs to explain around 85% or more of the variance balances reducing dimensionality and retaining information.

Step 6: Decide Number of Components to Retain

Calculate cumulative variance explained to determine the minimum number of PCs needed.

```
R Code
cumsum(explained_var)
```

Output

```
## [1]  0.6182781 0.8175993 0.9534195 1.0000000
```

If the first two PCs explain ove 80% or more of the variance, so retaining only these two components simplifies the dataset while preserving most of the information. This is the essential idea behind using principal components. Although there are only 4 variables in this dataset if there were 20 or so or even more you can see how parsing down the number of features to capture the essential information makes principal components useful.

Principal comonents may be used for visualization, clustering, or further analysis in place of using the original data with results giving valid and useful results. The essential meaning of the data is conserved in the principal components.

Step 7: Extract Principal Component Scores

We create a new dataset combining the original sample IDs and their scores on each PC.

R Code

```
pca_scores <- data.frame(Sample = food_data$Sample,
                         pca_result$x)
head(pca_scores)
```

```
Output
##   Sample         PC1         PC2         PC3         PC4
## 1      S1   0.5367754   0.9184948   0.41497708  -0.78132673
## 2      S2  -0.7923316   0.8557623  -0.39351366   0.27572718
## 3      S3   1.7779416  -0.8017569  -0.05707448   0.51032636
## 4      S4   0.6160880  -0.5976604   0.55505335  -0.40001119
## 5      S5   0.2283871  -0.9600334   0.72037265  -0.04511319
## 6      S6   2.6790260   0.4457812  -0.32839987   0.38807471
```

These scores represent where each sample lies along the new axes defined by PCA. For example, a sample with a high PC1 score and low PC2 score may have high Acidity and Sugar but low Bitterness, depending on the loadings. Samples with similar scores on the components tend to group together, meaning they have similar chemical characteristics. Large differences in scores between samples suggest stronger variation in their profiles. This transformed dataset is now ready to be used for visualization, clustering, or further analysis in a simplified, lower-dimensional space.

Step 8: Examine Loadings

Principal component loadings tell us how much each original variable contributes to each new principal component. A loading in Principal Component Analysis (PCA) is conceptually similar to a coefficient in a model.

```
R Code
loadings <- pca_result$rotation
loadings
```

```
Output
##                      PC1          PC2          PC3          PC4
## Acidity       0.5452908   -0.3000968   -0.4695369    0.6262068
## Sugar         0.4871204    0.5716077   -0.4473363   -0.4856631
## Aroma        -0.4820725   -0.4081374   -0.7110389   -0.3089555
## Bitterness    0.4826777   -0.6454691    0.2717516   -0.5258735
```

These values show the weight or importance of each variable in forming the new axes of variation. For example, in the loadings for PC1, Acidity has a value of 0.545, Sugar 0.487, Bitterness 0.483, and Aroma −0.482. Since the first three variables are all positive and relatively similar in size, and Aroma is similarly strong but negative, PC1 can be interpreted as an overall "flavor intensity" measure where higher scores indicate higher Acidity, Sugar, and Bitterness but lower Aroma. This suggests that samples with high PC1 scores are intense and sharp, while those with low scores are milder and more aromatic.

For PC2, Sugar has a strong positive loading of 0.572, while Bitterness has a strong negative loading of −0.645. This contrast implies that PC2 represents a tradeoff between sweetness and bitterness. Samples scoring high on PC2 are sweeter and less bitter, while those with low PC2 scores are more bitter and less sweet. By examining the sign and size of each variable's loading, we can understand what each component represents and how it captures different patterns or oppositions in the dataset. These interpretations are key for making sense of the reduced dimensions in PC

Step 9: Manual Calculation of PC Scores

To verify PCA computations, we can manually calculate a PC score for any observation by multiplying the standardized variable values by their corresponding loadings and summing. This is good to do onece because otherwise the concept of PCA can be very abstract.

```
R Code
obs1 <- features_scaled[1, ]
pc1_loadings <- loadings[, 1]
manual_PC1 <- sum(obs1 * pc1_loadings)


obs1
```

```
Output
##      Acidity       Sugar       Aroma  Bitterness
## -0.6670578   0.9803201  -0.6873064   0.1898791
```

```
R Code
pc1_loadings
```

```
Output
##      Acidity       Sugar       Aroma  Bitterness
##    0.5452908   0.4871204  -0.4820725   0.4826777
```

```
R Code
manual_PC1
```

```
Output
## [1] 0.5367754
```

To manually compute the PC1 score for this observation, we multiply each standardized variable by its corresponding PC1 loading and then add the results together.

Here are the values:

1. The standardized value for Acidity is −0.667, and its PC1 loading is 0.545. So we calculate −0.667 × 0.545 = −0.363015.

2. The standardized value for Sugar is 0.980, and its PC1 loading is 0.487. So we calculate 0.980 × 0.487 = 0.47726.

3. The standardized value for Aroma is −0.687, and its PC1 loading is −0.482. So we calculate −0.687 × −0.482 = 0.331434.

4. The standardized value for Bitterness is 0.190, and its PC1 loading is 0.483. So we calculate 0.190 × 0.483 = 0.09177.

Now we add all four of these values together:

PC1 score = −0.363015 + 0.47726 + 0.331434 + 0.09177 = 0.53745

So the PC1 score for this observation is approximately 0.537. This score tells us that this particular food sample is just above average on the new PC1 axis, which likely represents a combined intensity pattern involving all four original variables.

Step 10: Visualize Principal Components

We can plot samples on the first two PCs to observe clustering or outliers.

R Code

```
plot(pca_result$x[, 1], pca_result$x[, 2],
  xlab = "PC1",
  ylab = "PC2", main = "PCA Score Plot", pch = 19,
  col = "#3D5A80"
)
text(pca_result$x[, 1], pca_result$x[, 2],
  labels = food_data$Sample, pos = 3
)
```

PCA Score Plot

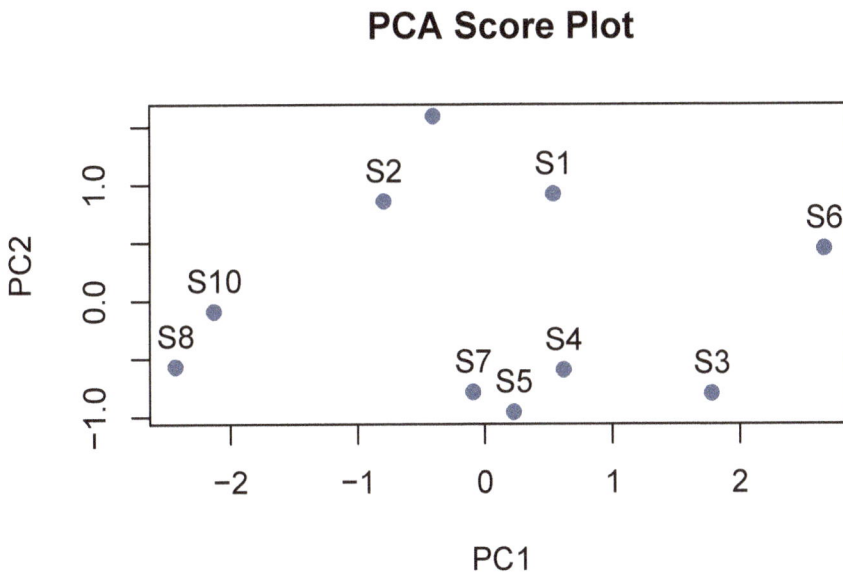

This PCA Score Plot shows how each food sample (labeled S1 through S10) is positioned based on the first two principal components (PC1 and PC2). Each dot represents one sample, plotted according to its scores on PC1 (horizontal axis) and PC2 (vertical axis). These principal components summarize the main patterns in the original chemical variables (like Acidity, Sugar, Aroma, and Bitterness).

Here's what the plot tells us:

PC1 separates samples from left to right. Samples far to the right (like S3 and S6) have high PC1 scores, which means they had higher overall values on the combination of original variables that made up PC1. Those far to the left (like S10 and S8) had lower values on that combined dimension.

PC2 separates samples vertically. Samples like S2 and S1 are higher on PC2, suggesting that their values differ in a second important way captured by PC2—possibly a trade-off or contrast between certain variables (like high aroma but low bitterness, for example). Samples lower on PC2, like S7, S5, and S8, differ in the opposite direction.

Samples close together, like S4, S5, and S7, have similar scores on both PC1 and PC2. That means their original chemical profiles were fairly similar across the board. Although we are not doing cluster analysis here technically this is why principal components can be used often for cluster analysis.

Samples are sometimes far apart, like S3 and S10, and have very different profiles—they don't share similar values in the original variables that PC1 and PC2 represent.

Wrap-Up

Principal Component Analysis (PCA) is a powerful technique to simplify complex datasets by creating new variables called principal components. PCA reduces the complexity of data, making it simpler to interpret and analyze without losing essential information.

Exercises

Principal Components Analysis

In this exercise you can practice how Principal Component Analysis (PCA) can be used to simplify and understand complex datasets involving multiple related variables.

Dataset: Plant Nutrients

This dataset contains measurements of key nutrient concentrations—Nitrogen, Phosphorus, Potassium, Calcium, and Magnesium—across 12 different plants. We will use these variables to perform Principal Component Analysis (PCA) and identify underlying patterns in nutrient profiles.

```
R Code
plant_data <- data.frame(
  Plant = c(
    "Plant1", "Plant2", "Plant3", "Plant4",
    "Plant5", "Plant6", "Plant7", "Plant8",
    "Plant9", "Plant10", "Plant11", "Plant12"
  ),
  Nitrogen = c(
    3.5, 2.9, 4.1, 3.7, 3.2, 3.9, 4.0,
    2.8, 3.1, 3.6, 3.3, 4.2
  ),
  Phosphorus = c(
    1.2, 1.0, 1.3, 1.1, 1.0, 1.4,
    1.3, 1.1, 1.2, 1.3, 1.0, 1.5
  ),
  Potassium = c(
    2.5, 2.2, 2.7, 2.6, 2.3, 2.8, 2.9,
    2.1, 2.4, 2.7, 2.2, 3.0
  ),
  Calcium = c(
    0.8, 0.9, 0.7, 0.8, 0.9, 0.7, 0.6,
    1.0, 0.8, 0.7, 0.9, 0.6
  ),
  Magnesium = c(
    0.5, 0.6, 0.4, 0.5, 0.6, 0.5, 0.4,
    0.7, 0.5, 0.4, 0.6, 0.4
  )
)
```

1. Print the data frame to inspect the plant nutrient data.

2. Select only the numeric nutrient columns (exclude the "Plant" identifier) for PCA analysis.

3. Normalize the numeric data using z-score standardization (scale function). Show your code and output.

4. Perform PCA on the normalized data using `prcomp()`. Set appropriate parameters considering the data is already scaled.

5. Create a scree plot showing the proportion of variance explained by each principal component.

6. Calculate and print the cumulative proportion of variance explained by the components.

7. Decide how many principal components to retain based on the scree plot and cumulative variance.

8. Extract and print the loadings (rotation matrix) of the principal components.

9. Create a new data frame combining the original plant data and the PCA scores for each plant.

10. Print the combined data frame showing plant identifiers and their scores on the retained principal components.

Dataset : Car Performance Attributes

This dataset contains key performance measurements of 10 different cars, including horsepower, weight, acceleration, and miles per gallon (MPG). We will use these variables to perform Principal Component Analysis (PCA) and explore patterns in the data.

R Code

```
car_data <- data.frame(
  Car = c(
    "Car1", "Car2", "Car3", "Car4",
    "Car5", "Car6", "Car7", "Car8",
    "Car9", "Car10"
  ),
  Horsepower = c(
    130, 165, 150, 140, 198,
    220, 215, 225, 190, 170
  ),
  Weight = c(
    3504, 3693, 3436, 3433, 4341,
    4354, 4312, 4425, 3850, 3563
  ),
  Acceleration = c(
    12.0, 11.5, 11.0, 12.0,
    10.0, 9.5, 9.0, 8.5, 10.5, 11.0
  ),
  MPG = c(
    18.0, 15.0, 18.0, 16.0, 15.0, 14.0,
    14.0, 14.0, 15.0, 15.0
  )
)
```

11. Print the `car_data` data frame to view the attributes of each car.

12. Extract only the numeric columns (`Horsepower`, `Weight`, `Acceleration`, `MPG`) for PCA.

13. Standardize the numeric data using z-score normalization. Show the R code and resulting standardized data.

14. Perform PCA on the standardized data with `prcomp()`, specifying the appropriate parameters.

15. Create a scree plot to visualize the variance explained by each principal component.

16. Calculate and display the cumulative variance explained by the principal components.

17. Based on the scree plot and cumulative variance, decide how many components to retain for analysis.

18. Extract and print the loadings to understand how each original variable contributes to the principal components.

19. Combine the original `car_data` with the PCA scores for each car, creating a new data frame.

20. Print the new combined data frame showing each car's identifier and its scores on the retained principal components.

Lab 5

Distance Calculations

Introduction

In many data analysis tasks such as clustering or classification, it is important to measure how similar or different data points are from one another. This similarity is quantified using distance metrics. In this lab, you will learn how to calculate Euclidean distances between observations in a dataset. Euclidean distance is simply the same distance formula you used in high school geometry to find the shortest distance between two points and it expands to n-space.

Lesson Steps

Step 1: Create the Data

For this tutorial, we will create a simple employee dataset with the variables EmployeeID, Department, YearsExperience, and Salary.

R Code

```r
data <- data.frame(
  EmployeeID = c(
    101, 102, 103, 104, 105, 106,
    107, 108, 109, 110
  ),
  Department = c(
    "Sales", "Marketing", "IT",
    "HR", "Sales", "IT", "Marketing", "HR", "Sales", "IT"
  ),
  YearsExperience = c(2, 5, 7, 3, 8, 4, 6, 1, 10, 9),
  Salary = c(
    48000, 58000, 75000, 52000, 69000,
    60000, 62000, 45000, 80000, 82000
  )
)

head(data)
```

Output

```
##   EmployeeID Department YearsExperience Salary
## 1        101      Sales               2  48000
## 2        102  Marketing               5  58000
## 3        103         IT               7  75000
## 4        104         HR               3  52000
## 5        105      Sales               8  69000
## 6        106         IT               4  60000
```

Step 2: Set Data Types

You always need to ensure that the variables used for distance calculations are stored as numeric types. Distance calculations involve mathematical operations that only work on numeric data. Sometimes when data is imported, variables might be read as characters or factors, especially if the data contains missing or malformed entries. To avoid problems, convert all columns explicitly to numeric.

```
R Code
data_numeric <- data.frame(
  YearsExperience = as.numeric(data$YearsExperience),
  Salary = as.numeric(data$Salary)
)


head(data_numeric)
```

```
Output
##   YearsExperience Salary
## 1               2  48000
## 2               5  58000
## 3               7  75000
## 4               3  52000
## 5               8  69000
## 6               4  60000
```

Step 3: Compute Distance Matrix (Raw Data)

Once the data is numeric, you can calculate the distances between every pair of observations. A distance matrix contains these pairwise distances, which are fundamental inputs for clustering and similarity analysis.

The Euclidean distance is the straight-line distance between two points in multidimensional space and is calculated as the square root of the sum of squared differences in each dimension. In R, the dist() function with method "euclidean" computes this distance efficiently for all pairs of points. Converting the resulting object to a matrix format allows easier visualization and interpretation of the distances.

```
R Code
dist_raw <- dist(data_numeric, method = "euclidean")
dist_raw_matrix <- as.matrix(dist_raw)


# Print part of matrix
print(round(dist_raw_matrix[1:5, 1:5], 2))
```

```
Output
##          1      2      3      4      5
## 1       0  10000  27000   4000  21000
## 2   10000      0  17000   6000  11000
## 3   27000  17000      0  23000   6000
## 4    4000   6000  23000      0  17000
## 5   21000  11000   6000  17000      0
```

At this point, remember that the distances you see are influenced by the scale of each variable. Variables with larger numerical ranges will dominate the distance calculations.

Step 4: Normalize the Data

Because variables can have different units and ranges — for example, YearsExperience might range from 1 to 10 years, while Salary can range from 45,000 to 82,000 dollars — variables with larger scales will disproportionately affect the distance calculations. To avoid this, it is necessary to normalize the data so that each variable has a mean of zero and a standard deviation of one. This transformation, called z-score standardization, rescales the variables to have the same scale, ensuring that each variable contributes equally to the distance calculations. After normalization, the values indicate how many standard deviations each observation is from the variable's mean.

R Code
```
data_normalized <- scale(data_numeric)
print(head(data_normalized))
```

Output
```
##         YearsExperience      Salary
## [1,]         -1.1560120 -1.1562671
## [2,]         -0.1651446 -0.3905273
## [3,]          0.4954337  0.9112303
## [4,]         -0.8257228 -0.8499712
## [5,]          0.8257228  0.4517865
## [6,]         -0.4954337 -0.2373793
```

Step 5: Compute Distance on Normalized Data

After normalizing the data, recalculate the distance matrix using the transformed values. This new distance matrix reflects the distances between observations after removing the effect of different variable scales. Calculating

distances on normalized data often results in more balanced and meaningful similarity measures that better reflect the overall patterns in the dataset.

```
R Code
dist_normalized <- dist(data_normalized, method = "euclidean")
dist_normalized_matrix <- as.matrix(dist_normalized)
print(round(dist_normalized_matrix[1:5, 1:5], 2))
```

```
Output
##         1     2     3     4     5
## 1  0.00  1.25  2.65  0.45  2.55
## 2  1.25  0.00  1.46  0.80  1.30
## 3  2.65  1.46  0.00  2.20  0.57
## 4  0.45  0.80  2.20  0.00  2.10
## 5  2.55  1.30  0.57  2.10  0.00
```

Step 6: Compare Results

To understand the effect of normalization, compare the distance matrices
computed on raw and normalized data (both printed above). By looking at
the first few rows and columns of each matrix, you can observe how distances change after normalization. Typically, distances based on raw data
may be skewed by variables with larger scales, while distances based on normalized data reflect a more balanced contribution from all variables. This
comparison helps build intuition about the importance of normalization in
analyses that rely on distance measures.

Wrap-Up

Distance metrics allow us to quantify how similar or different observations are. The Euclidean distance measures straight-line distance between points in multidimensional space. When variables differ greatly in scale, raw distance calculations can be misleading because variables with larger ranges dominate. Normalizing the data by centering to mean zero and scaling to unit variance ensures all variables contribute fairly to the distances.

Exercises

Distance Calculations

In this exercise set, you will practice creating datasets, computing distance matrices, normalizing data, and interpreting the results

Dataset 1: Customer Demographics and Spending

Create the following dataset representing customers, their age, annual income (in thousands), and spending score (a measure of their engagement):

```
R Code
customers <- data.frame(
  CustomerID = 1:10,
  Age = c(22, 45, 25, 35, 52, 23, 40, 60, 48, 30),
  Income = c(35, 85, 40, 60, 90, 38, 75, 100, 80, 50),
  SpendingScore = c(60, 40, 65, 50, 30, 70, 45,
                    20, 35, 55)
)
```

1. Show the first six rows of the `customers` dataset.

2. Compute the Euclidean distance matrix using all numeric columns except `CustomerID`. Display the full matrix.

3. Normalize the numeric variables (Age, Income, SpendingScore) using z-score standardization. Show the first six rows of the normalized data.

4. Calculate the Euclidean distance matrix on the normalized data. Display the first 5 rows and columns of the matrix rounded to two decimals.

5. Compare the distance matrices from raw and normalized data. De-

scribe one key difference you observe between the two matrices and explain why normalization changes the distances.

Dataset 2: Product Features

Create a dataset representing 8 products with three numeric features indicating their quality, durability, and price (all scaled 1 to 10):

```
R Code
products <- data.frame(
  ProductID = 1:8,
  Quality = c(8, 6, 9, 5, 7, 8, 6, 7),
  Durability = c(7, 5, 8, 6, 7, 6, 5, 7),
  Price = c(6, 4, 9, 5, 7, 8, 4, 6)
)
```

6. Display the structure (str()) of the products dataset.

7. Calculate the Euclidean distance matrix based on the raw numeric features (Quality, Durability, Price). Show the distance between Product 1 and all other products.

8. Normalize the numeric features and display the normalized data.

9. Compute the Euclidean distance matrix on the normalized features. Show the distances between Product 1 and all others rounded to two decimals.

10. Based on the normalized distances, which product is most similar to Product 1? Explain your reasoning based on the distance values.

Lab 6

Hierarchical Clustering

This lab guides you through hierarchical clustering in R. Hierarchical clustering is a method used to group similar objects based on their characteristics by building a tree-like structure called a dendrogram. The process starts with each object as its own cluster and then successively merges the closest clusters until all objects are combined into a single group. This allows you to explore natural groupings in your data.

Lesson Step

Step 1: Load the Data

We start by creating a sample dataset with measurements on physical objects. The data frame includes four numeric variables m1, m2, m3, and m4.

```
R Code
# Create sample dataset directly in R
set.seed(123)  # for reproducibility
data <- data.frame(
  m1 = c(5.1, 4.9, 4.7, 6.0, 5.4, 5.0, 5.5, 6.3, 5.8, 6.1,
         5.6, 5.7, 6.4, 5.3, 5.8, 6.5, 5.0, 5.2, 6.1, 5.9),
  m2 = c(3.5, 3.0, 3.2, 2.9, 3.7, 3.6, 3.8, 3.3, 2.7, 3.0,
         2.9, 2.8, 3.2, 3.5, 2.6, 3.0, 3.4, 3.4, 2.5, 3.2),
  m3 = c(1.4, 1.4, 1.3, 4.5, 1.5, 1.4, 1.3, 4.9, 4.0, 4.7,
         3.6, 4.5, 5.0, 1.4, 1.2, 5.2, 1.5, 1.5, 5.9, 4.8),
  m4 = c(0.2, 0.2, 0.2, 1.5, 0.2, 0.2, 0.2, 1.5, 1.3, 1.4,
         1.2, 1.5, 2.0, 0.2, 0.2, 2.0, 0.2, 0.2, 2.1, 1.8)
)

head(data)
```

```
Output
##     m1  m2  m3  m4
## 1 5.1 3.5 1.4 0.2
## 2 4.9 3.0 1.4 0.2
## 3 4.7 3.2 1.3 0.2
## 4 6.0 2.9 4.5 1.5
## 5 5.4 3.7 1.5 0.2
## 6 5.0 3.6 1.4 0.2
```

Step 2: Set Data Types

Make sure all data is numeric. Since the data was created as numeric, this is a confirmation step. Use `lapply()` to ensure all fields are numeric and `str()` to confirm.

R Code
```
data <- data.frame(lapply(data, as.numeric))


# Check data type and structure
str(data)
```

Output
```
## 'data.frame':    20 obs. of  4 variables:
##  $ m1: num  5.1 4.9 4.7 6 5.4 5 5.5 6.3 5.8 6.1 ...
##  $ m2: num  3.5 3 3.2 2.9 3.7 3.6 3.8 3.3 2.7 3 ...
##  $ m3: num  1.4 1.4 1.3 4.5 1.5 1.4 1.3 4.9 4 4.7 ...
##  $ m4: num  0.2 0.2 0.2 1.5 0.2 0.2 0.2 1.5 1.3 1.4 ...
```

Step 3: Normalize the Data

This data has four variables, `m1`, `m2`, `m3` and `m4` all of which are on different scales, so normalization ensures each variable contributes equally. In R, we use `scale()` when it is desired to convert the entire data frame to standard normal scores.

R Code
```
data_normalized <- scale(data)
```

Step 4: Check Normalized Data

Before proceeding since clustering is highly sensitive to scale double check that the data are in fact normalized. Use the `head()` function to view part of the data.

R Code

```
head(data_normalized)
```

Output

```
##                 m1           m2           m3           m4
## [1,]  -0.9709343   0.9248221  -0.9378538  -0.9335403
## [2,]  -1.3479962  -0.4352104  -0.9378538  -0.9335403
## [3,]  -1.7250581   0.1088026  -0.9946935  -0.9335403
## [4,]   0.7258441  -0.7072169   0.8241746   0.7638057
## [5,]  -0.4053415   1.4688351  -0.8810142  -0.9335403
## [6,]  -1.1594653   1.1968286  -0.9378538  -0.9335403
```

Results show the normalized data. The data is now ready to use.

Step 5: Compute Distances

In hierarchical clustering, we need to group data points based on how similar or different they are from each other. To do that, the algorithm first needs to measure the distance between every pair of points in the dataset. This step is called computing the distance matrix. The distance matrix tells the algorithm which points are close together and which are farther apart, which is essential for building the hierarchy of clusters.

We often use a method called Euclidean distance, which measures the straight-line distance between two points. Before calculating these distances, the data is usually normalized so that all variables contribute equally to the distance measurement.

To compute distance, we use function `dist()` which is in base R (no need for additional packages).

> **R Code**
> ```
> dist_matrix <- dist(data_normalized, method = "euclidean")
> ```

Step 6: View Distance Matrix

The distance matrix shows distances between each pair of data points. To view the distance matrix we want to convert the data frame object to a matrix and then view part of it (because otherwise it is large and unwieldy).

> **R Code**
> ```
> dist_matrix_view <- as.matrix(dist_matrix)
> round(dist_matrix_view[1:5, 1:5], 2)
> ```

> **Output**
> ```
> ##       1    2    3    4    5
> ## 1  0.00 1.41 1.11 3.40 0.79
> ## 2  1.41 0.00 0.66 3.22 2.13
> ## 3  1.11 0.66 0.00 3.59 1.90
> ## 4  3.40 3.22 3.59 0.00 3.44
> ## 5  0.79 2.13 1.90 3.44 0.00
> ```

The partial printout of the distance matrix is shown below. Row 1 column 1 is the distance of observation 1 to observation 1 which is of course zero. Row 1 column 2 is the distance from observation 1 to observation 2 which could be computed from the standardized data using the Euclidean distance formula. Row 2 column 1 is the same as row 1 column 2 as the matrix is symmetric across the diagonal. These distance values are what the clustering algorithm will use to determine structure of the data.

Step 7: Run Hierarchical Clustering

To run the clustering algorithm, we will use function `hclust()` on the distance matrix. This function takes a distance matrix (like the one created by `dist()`) and performs hierarchical clustering to build a cluster tree (dendrogram). The default method is single linkage (linkage is described in the textbook in Chapter 4).

```
R Code
hc_single <- hclust(dist_matrix, method = "single")
hc_single
```

```
Output
##
## Call:
## hclust(d = dist_matrix, method = "single")
##
## Cluster method   : single
## Distance         : euclidean
## Number of objects: 20
```

Examining the output just gives basic information about the clustering but otherwise is not informative about the actual results.

Step 8: View Dendrogram

To actually see the results of a hierarchical clustering a visual output known as a dendrogram is used. A dendrogram is a tree-like diagram that shows how data points are grouped together in hierarchical clustering. It visually represents the order and distance at which clusters are merged, helping you see patterns and decide how many clusters to keep.

To produce a dendrogram in R use function `plot()` and feed in the result output from the clustering function. The function will recognize the input is a clustering object from hierarchical clustering and produce a dendrogram plot. Additional optional parameters such as a title and axis labels can be applied.

R Code
```
plot(hc_single, main = "Dendrogram (Single Linkage)",
     xlab = "", sub = "", cex = 0.8)
```

Dendrogram (Single Linkage)

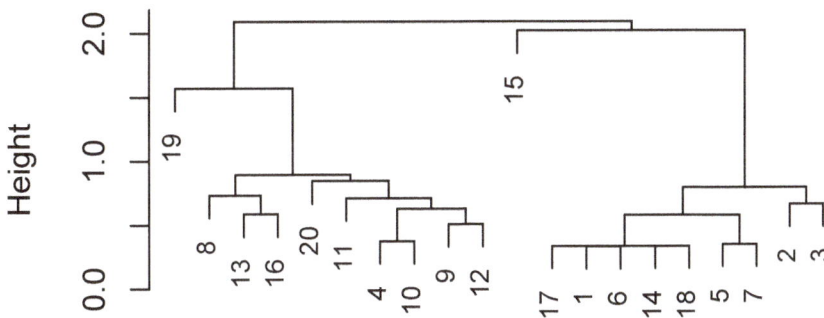

The result produced is a dendrogram plot.

This dendrogram shows how the data points are grouped based on similarity using single linkage clustering. Points that are joined lower on the diagram, like 10 and 15, are more similar to each other, while those that join higher up are less similar. The height of each merge shows how different the clusters are when they combine. By drawing a horizontal line across the dendrogram (for example, at height 1.5), you can choose how many clusters to keep—lower cuts give more clusters, higher cuts give fewer.

Step 9: Consider Other Linkage Methods

Different linkage methods (discussed in Chapter 4 of the main text) in hierarchical clustering changes how clusters are formed. While single linkage joins clusters based on the closest pair of points (the shortest distance between them), Ward's method focuses on minimizing the total variance within clusters. In other words, Ward's method tries to keep the clusters as compact and balanced as possible.

The reason you might choose Ward's method is that it tends to produce more evenly sized, well-separated clusters, especially when working with continuous, normalized data. In contrast, single linkage can lead to long, chain-like clusters where one point gets added at a time, which may not always reflect meaningful groupings. So, if you want clearer and more compact clusters, Ward's method is usually a better choice.

Let's redo the clustering using Ward's method. To do this simply change the method parameter in the `hclust` function.

```
R Code
hc_ward <- hclust(dist_matrix, method = "ward.D2")


# Plot dendrogram for Ward's linkage
plot(hc_ward, main = "Dendrogram (Ward Linkage)",
     xlab = "", sub = "", cex = 0.8)
```

Dendrogram (Ward Linkage)

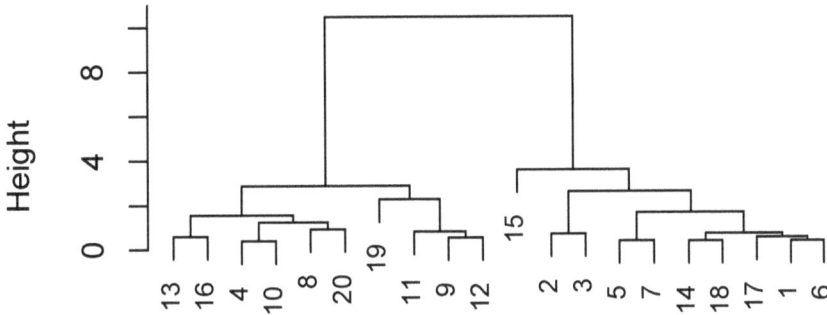

The dendrogram produced by Ward linkage shows more well-defined clusters and is easier to interpret.

Step 10: Determining Optimal Clustering

Remember that clustering is an unsupervised exploratory technique for finding initial structure in data typically when little is known about how the data groups together. It is not a hard defined technique where one specific best answer prevails. Typically, you will explore different linkages and consult a domain expert (knowledge about the data content if you are not) to finalize the decision on the best clustering for a particular data set.

Wrap-Up

The lesson demonstrated how to perform hierarchical clustering using different linkage methods, such as single linkage and Ward's method. You practiced visualizing the resulting cluster structures with dendrograms, which provide a clear view of how clusters form at different similarity levels. Finally, you gained an understanding of how the choice of linkage method influences the shape and interpretation of the clusters.

Lab 6 Exercises

Hierarchical Clustering Exercises

This exercise guides you through hierarchical clustering. You will normalize variables on different scales, compute Euclidean distances, run hierarchical clustering with different linkage methods, and visualize cluster structures with dendrograms.

Dataset 1: Synthetic Plant Measurements

```
R Code
set.seed(101)
plant_data <- data.frame(
  Height = rnorm(15, mean = 50, sd = 10),
  Leaf_Length = rnorm(15, mean = 20, sd = 5),
  Leaf_Width = rnorm(15, mean = 5, sd = 1.5),
  Petal_Count = sample(3:10, 15, replace = TRUE)
)
```

1. Show the first six rows of the plant data. What are the variables included?
2. Normalize the data using the `scale()` function. Display the first six rows of the normalized data.
3. Compute the Euclidean distance matrix on the normalized data and show the distance matrix for the first 5 rows and columns.
4. Perform hierarchical clustering using single linkage on the distance matrix. Print the result object.
5. Plot the dendrogram for the single linkage clustering. Describe one pattern you observe from the dendrogram.

Dataset 2: Customer Purchasing Behavior

```
R Code
set.seed(202)
customer_data <- data.frame(
  Purchases_Last_Month = sample(1:20, 20, replace = TRUE),
  Average_Spend = rnorm(20, mean = 100, sd = 30),
  Visit_Frequency = rpois(20, lambda = 5),
  Loyalty_Score = runif(20, min = 0, max = 1)
)
```

6. Show the first six rows of the customer data. Which variables are continuous and which are counts?

7. Normalize the customer data and display the first six rows of the scaled data.

8. Compute the Euclidean distance matrix on the normalized customer data and display the distances for the first 5 rows and columns.

9. Perform hierarchical clustering using Ward's method (method = "ward.D2") on the distance matrix. Print the result object.

10. Plot the dendrogram for the Ward linkage clustering. How does the cluster structure compare to what you would expect if you cut the dendrogram at a medium height?

Dataset 3: Movie Ratings by Viewers

R Code

```
set.seed(303)
movie_data <- data.frame(
  Action_Rating = sample(1:10, 12, replace = TRUE),
  Comedy_Rating = sample(1:10, 12, replace = TRUE),
  Drama_Rating = sample(1:10, 12, replace = TRUE)
)
```

11. Normalize the movie ratings data and compute the Euclidean distance matrix. Show the distance matrix for the first 5 rows and columns.

12. Perform hierarchical clustering using average linkage and plot the dendrogram. Which two movies are closest according to the dendrogram?

Lab 7

K-Means Clustering

Clustering is an unsupervised machine learning technique used to group similar data points together based on their characteristics (measured in distance). Among the most popular clustering methods is k-means clustering, which organizes data into k distinct clusters using distance-based optimization.

In this lab, we will walk through the full process of k-means clustering. This includes data preparation, normalization, silhouette analysis to determine the best k, applying k-means, and visualizing the results.

Lesson Steps

Step 1: Create the Data

We will generate a synthetic dataset here for demonstration purposes. This dataset simulates salary-related variables for clustering.

R Code

```
set.seed(123)   # For reproducibility


# Create synthetic dataset
data <- data.frame(

  # Random salaries (normal dist)
  Salary = round(rnorm(100, mean = 60000, sd = 15000), 0),

  # Random experience (uniform dist)
  Years_Experience = round(runif(100, min = 0, max = 20), 1),

  # Random ages (normal dist)
  Age = round(rnorm(100, mean = 35, sd = 10), 0)
)


head(data)
```

Output

```
##    Salary Years_Experience Age
## 1   51593              4.8  43
## 2   56547             19.2  43
## 3   83381             12.0  38
## 4   61058             10.3  25
## 5   61939              8.1  34
## 6   85726             17.6  32
```

Step 2: Set Data Types

Clustering requires that data is numeric. Make sure all the data is all numeric by applying function `lapply` to the data and view the results to be sure using function `str()`.

```
R Code
# Ensure all columns are numeric


data <- data.frame(lapply(data, as.numeric))
```

Step 3: Normalize the Data

In k-means clustering, it's important to normalize the data because the algorithm relies on distance calculations (typically Euclidean distance) to group data points. If the features are on different scales—such as income in the thousands and age in the tens—those with larger scales will dominate the clustering process, regardless of their actual importance.

The line `data_normalized <- scale(data)` standardizes each variable by subtracting the mean and dividing by the standard deviation, ensuring that all features have the same scale (mean 0 and standard deviation 1). This allows each feature to contribute equally to the clustering, leading to more meaningful and unbiased results.

```
R Code
# Standardize the data


data_normalized <- scale(data)


# Check normalized data


head(data_normalized)
```

```
Output
##           Salary Years_Experience       Age
## [1,] -0.71303714      -0.8363730  0.8390334
## [2,] -0.35122690       1.6120457  0.8390334
## [3,]  1.60856644       0.3878363  0.3052971
## [4,] -0.02177069       0.0987869 -1.0824171
## [5,]  0.04257223      -0.2752771 -0.1216919
## [6,]  1.77983108       1.3399992 -0.3351864
```

The data is normalized as shown above.

Step 4: Check Silhouette Scores

K-means clustering requires you to choose the number of clusters (K) in advance, but in real-world data, we often don't know what the best K is. Trying different values of K and checking their performance helps us make a more informed choice instead of guessing.

To compare them, we use a metric called a silhouette score. This score tells us how well each point fits in its own cluster and how far away it is from other clusters. It ranges from -1 to 1. A higher score means the clusters are well-separated and clearly defined.

By checking the average silhouette score for each K, we can see which number of clusters gives the best overall fit. This helps us choose a K that gives strong, meaningful groupings instead of just guessing. To do this in R we use the code here.

R Code
```
# Install if not already installed


options(repos = c(CRAN = "https://cran.r-project.org"))
install.packages("cluster")
install.packages("factoextra")
library(cluster)
library(factoextra)
```

R Code
```
# Try K from 2 to 6 and compute average silhouette width

silhouette_scores <- sapply(2:6, function(k) {
  km <- kmeans(data_normalized, centers = k, nstart = 25)
  ss <- silhouette(km$cluster, dist(data_normalized))
  mean(ss[, 3])  # Average silhouette width
})


# Display scores
silhouette_scores
```

Output
```
## [1] 0.2545153 0.2755178 0.2983694 0.3236242 0.3435743
```

This shows the average silhouette scores for k-means clustering with different numbers of clusters (K = 2 to 6). Each number corresponds to the average silhouette score for each K.

- K = 2 the score is 0.254 etc

Higher silhouette scores mean better-defined and more distinct clusters. Here, K = 6 has the highest score so we will use this for the number of clusters.

Step 5: Run K-Means

Function `kmeans` is part of base R and needs no packages installed. To use this function we use the normalized data and specify how many clusters as well as set a few other technical things in the code. From above we know the number of clusters is best set to 6.

`set.seed(42)` sets the random number generator seed. This ensures the results are reproducible—you'll get the same clustering every time you run the code. K-means involves random starting points, so without this, you might get different results each run.

Setting `nstart = 25`, k-means will run 25 times with different random initial centers and return the best result (lowest total within-cluster variation).

```
R Code
set.seed(42)
k_opt <- 6
kmeans_result <- kmeans(data_normalized,
   centers = k_opt, nstart = 25
)
```

The results are stored in `kmeans_result`.

Step 6: Visualize Clusters

To look at the clustering a scatterplot is necessary. Specialized plotting is available in the packages loaded in step 4 above (make sure these are loaded before running step 6 code). In addition, we will use package `ggplot2`.

PCA is used in this code not to perform clustering, but to make the k-means clustering results easier to visualize. When working with datasets that have many variables, it's difficult to plot or understand the data in more than two or three dimensions.

PCA (Principal Component Analysis) reduces the data to two principal components—PC1 and PC2—that capture most of the important patterns in the data. This allows us to create a 2D scatterplot where each point represents a data observation, colored by its assigned cluster.

Even though the k-means clustering was done in the full, high-dimensional space, PCA provides a way to see those groupings clearly in two dimensions. So, PCA is used here purely for visualization purposes, helping us better understand the clustering structure (although for this specific example there are only two variables we are using this, so it is easy to extend the code for larger datasets).

R Code

```
library(ggplot2)


pca <- prcomp(data_normalized)


df_plot <- data.frame(
  PC1 = pca$x[, 1],
  PC2 = pca$x[, 2],
  Cluster = factor(kmeans_result$cluster)
)


ggplot(df_plot, aes(x = PC1, y = PC2, color = Cluster)) +
  geom_point(size = 2) +
  labs(
    title = paste("K-Means Clusters (k =", k_opt, ")"),
    x = "PC1", y = "PC2"
  ) +
  theme_minimal()
```

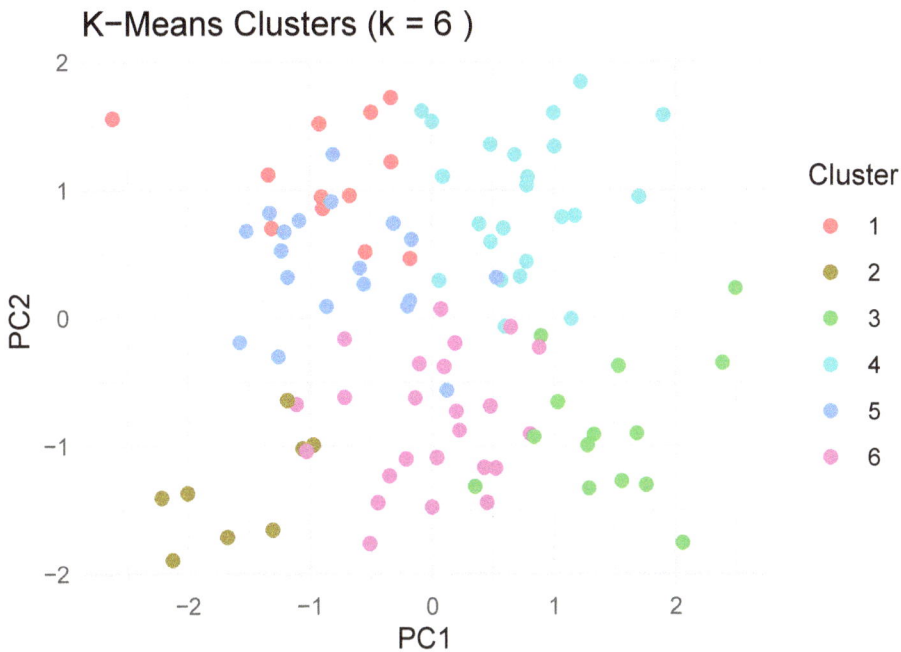

K–Means Clusters (k = 6)

The resulting plot shows the data nicely and cleanly clustered into 6 distinct clusters.

Step 7: Output Cluster Data

In order to make the results more useful it is possible to create an output file with the cluster results joined to the data. After running k-means, the results output produced has a cluster column. We can append this to the data for output and further analysis easily as coded below.

```
R Code
annotated_data <- data.frame(data,
   Cluster = kmeans_result$cluster
)
head(annotated_data)
```

```
Output
##    Salary Years_Experience Age Cluster
## 1  51593             4.8  43       5
## 2  56547            19.2  43       6
## 3  83381            12.0  38       3
## 4  61058            10.3  25       4
## 5  61939             8.1  34       4
## 6  85726            17.6  32       3
```

Wrap-Up

In this lab, you applied the complete k-means clustering process—from creating and normalizing synthetic data, to choosing the best number of clusters using silhouette scores, and finally visualizing and exporting the results. You also saw how Principal Component Analysis (PCA) can simplify the visual interpretation of high-dimensional clustering output.

Exercises

K-Means Clustering

In this exercise set, you will practice creating datasets, normalizing them, determining the optimal number of clusters using silhouette scores, applying k-means, and visualizing the results.

Dataset 1: Fitness

```
R Code
fitness_data <- data.frame(

  # Steps per day
  Steps = c(
    3500, 4200, 3900, 8200, 7900, 8600,
    10200, 9800, 10800,
    3700, 4100, 4000, 8000, 8300, 8700,
    10000, 9500, 10500, 3850, 8200
  ),

  # Active minutes per day
  Active_Minutes = c(
    20, 25, 18, 45, 42, 47,
    65, 70, 68, 22, 24, 19, 44,
    46, 48, 66, 72, 69, 21, 43
  ),

  # Estimated calories burned
  Calories_Burned = c(
    180, 200, 170, 310, 290, 330,
    410, 400, 420, 190, 195, 175,
    300, 305, 315, 405, 395, 425,
    185, 295
  )
)
```

1. Use `str()` and `lapply()` to confirm all variables in `fitness_data` are numeric. Paste your code and output.
2. Normalize the dataset using `scale()`. Paste the code and the first 5 rows of the normalized data.

3. Run silhouette scoring for values of K from 2 to 5. Paste the average silhouette scores for each K. Which K is best?

4. Apply `kmeans()` to the normalized data using the best K. Paste the code used to generate the result.

5. Use `prcomp()` and `ggplot2` to create a scatterplot of the clusters using PC1 and PC2. Include the plot in your answer.

Dataset 2: Product Sales Data

R Code

```
sales_data <- data.frame(

  # Units sold
  Units_Sold = c(
    350, 370, 340, 520, 510,
    530, 640, 660, 630,
    360, 380, 355, 500, 515,
    525, 645, 655, 635, 345, 505
  ),


  # Units returned
  Returns = c(
    25, 22, 27, 18, 20, 19, 12, 10, 11,
    24, 23, 26, 17, 19, 18, 13, 11, 12,
    28, 16
  ),


  # Average customer rating (out of 5)
  Customer_Rating = c(
    3.6, 3.7, 3.5, 4.2, 4.0,
    4.1, 4.8, 4.9, 4.85,
    3.65, 3.75, 3.55, 4.3, 4.1,
    4.0, 4.95, 4.88, 4.9, 3.6, 4.15
  )
)
```

6. Check that all variables are numeric and then normalize the dataset. Paste your R code for both steps.

7. Calculate average silhouette scores for K = 2 to K = 6. Which value of K appears optimal? Paste the scores.

8. Use `kmeans()` on the normalized dataset with your selected K. What is the size of each cluster?
9. Visualize the k-means clusters with PCA and `ggplot2`. Paste the code and include the resulting plot.
10. Add the cluster results back to the original dataset. Paste the first few rows of the annotated dataset.

Lab 8

Logistic Regression

Logistic regression is a statistical modeling approach used when the outcome variable is categorical, typically binary. It is often used in data mining as a basic classification method for categorizing features. Through data preparation, visualization, model fitting, probability prediction, and evaluation metrics, this lesson demonstrates the complete workflow for building and assessing a simple logistic regression model.

Lesson Steps

Step 1: Load the Data

To start, we need to get our data into R. Here we'll type the data directly into R for simplicity.

```
R Code
data <- data.frame(
  Height = c(47, 48, 49, 50, 51, 52, 53, 54, 55, 56,
             57, 58, 59, 60, 61, 62, 63, 64, 65, 66,
             67, 68, 69, 70, 71, 54, 55, 56, 59, 60),
  Adult_Binary = c(0, 0, 0, 0, 0, 0, 0, 0, 0, 0,
                   0, 1, 1, 1, 1, 1, 1, 1, 1, 1,
                   1, 1, 1, 1, 1, 1, 1, 1, 0, 0)
)
```

Step 2: Visualize the Data with a Boxplot

Before running any model, we want to explore the data. In particular for
logistic regression, we wish to see a group separation that would warrant
using this type of model.

A boxplot showing how height differs between adults and non-adults would
be a good visual to do. If adults tend to have higher heights than non-adults,
it makes sense that height could predict adult status.

```
R Code
# Boxplot to compare heights adults vs. non-adults
boxplot(Height ~ Adult_Binary, data = data,
        xlab = "Adult Status", ylab = "Height (inches)",
        main = "Boxplot of Height by Adult Status",
        col = c("#3D5A80", "#EE6C4D"))
```

Boxplot of Height by Adult Status

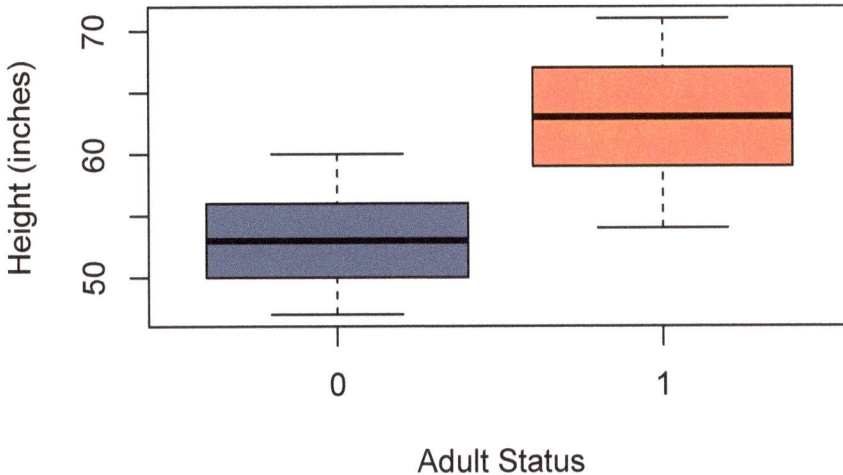

The resulting plot shows a clear distinction between child and adult height.

Step 4: Build the Logistic Regression Model

Now we create the model using R's `glm()` function."GLM" stands for Generalized Linear Model, and we use it with the binomial family to create a logistic regression model. This model will try to predict whether someone is an adult (Yes or No) based on their height. Note the specification of using `binomial` (this is important).

```
R Code
# Fit a logistic regression model
model <- glm(Adult_Binary ~ Height,
            data = data, family = binomial)
```

The model results are stored in the `model` object created.

Step 5: Look at the Model Summary

The `summary()` function shows us the model details, including the coefficients, and just needs the stored model object from step 4 as input. Let's just look at the coefficients here.

```
R Code
# Model summary
summary(model$coefficients)
```

```
Output
##      Min.  1st Qu.    Median      Mean  3rd Qu.      Max.
## -24.8948 -18.5617 -12.2287 -12.2287   -5.8956    0.4374
```

This summary shows the results of a logistic regression model predicting whether a person is an adult (`Adult_Binary`) based on their height.

The intercept is around -25 and the height coefficient is about 0.44. The logistic model can be written from this.

Step 6: Predict the Probability for Each Person

The model can now predict the probability that each person in the data is an adult.

These probabilities are numbers between 0 and 1, where a number close to 1 means "very likely an adult," and close to 0 means "not likely."

We usually want a simple Yes/No prediction instead of a decimal probability. We do this by choosing a cutoff threshold—commonly 0.5. If the predicted probability is greater than 0.5, we say "Yes", otherwise we say "No".

Let's code this in R and look at the results.

```
R Code
# Add a column of predicted probabilities to the dataset
data$predicted_prob <- predict(model, type = "response")


# Turn predicted probabilities into class labels
data$predicted_class <- ifelse(data$predicted_prob > 0.5,
                               "Yes", "No")


as.matrix(data$predicted_prob)
```

Output	
##	[,1]
## [1,]	0.01292745
## [2,]	0.01988009
## [3,]	0.03045661
## [4,]	0.04639365
## [5,]	0.07006741
## [6,]	0.10449764
## [7,]	0.15306174
## [8,]	0.21868390
## [9,]	0.30239509
## [10,]	0.40167651
## [11,]	0.50973613
## [12,]	0.61689351
## [13,]	0.71378069
## [14,]	0.79433414
## [15,]	0.85676602
## [16,]	0.90257064
## [17,]	0.93484144
## [18,]	0.95693345
## [19,]	0.97176142
## [20,]	0.98158233
## [21,]	0.98802976
## [22,]	0.99223800
## [23,]	0.99497433
## [24,]	0.99674918
## [25,]	0.99789855
## [26,]	0.21868390
## [27,]	0.30239509
## [28,]	0.40167651
## [29,]	0.71378069

```
## [30,] 0.79433414
```

```
as.matrix(data$predicted_class)
```

```
##         [,1]
## [1,]  "No"
## [2,]  "No"
## [3,]  "No"
## [4,]  "No"
## [5,]  "No"
## [6,]  "No"
## [7,]  "No"
## [8,]  "No"
## [9,]  "No"
## [10,] "No"
## [11,] "Yes"
## [12,] "Yes"
## [13,] "Yes"
## [14,] "Yes"
## [15,] "Yes"
## [16,] "Yes"
## [17,] "Yes"
## [18,] "Yes"
## [19,] "Yes"
## [20,] "Yes"
## [21,] "Yes"
## [22,] "Yes"
## [23,] "Yes"
```

```
## [24,] "Yes"
## [25,] "Yes"
## [26,] "No"
## [27,] "No"
## [28,] "No"
## [29,] "Yes"
## [30,] "Yes"
```

The first output are the actual probability values from the model (if the coefficients were used and the data were substituted into the resulting equation, this is what would be obtained).

These are unwieldy to work with, so instead, using a cutoff value of 0.5, we translate these into Yes or No categories (adult or not).

Step 7: Make a Confusion Matrix

A confusion matrix is a table that compares the model's predictions to the actual values. It shows how many people were predicted correctly or incorrectly.

We can use our results and simply create a table output showing this.

```
R Code
# Create a confusion matrix
table(Predicted = data$predicted_class,
      Actual = data$Adult_Binary)
```

```
##           Actual
## Predicted  0  1
##       No  10  3
##      Yes   3 14
```

The results show there is one misclassification in the predicted values when compared to the actual data values for whether or not the individual is an adult.

Step 8: Calculate Model Accuracy

Accuracy is the percentage of predictions that the model got right. It's a basic way to evaluate how well your model works.

Of the 30 data observations used here, 24 are predicted accurately by the model (with one misclassification) which is an 80% accuracy rate.

Wrap-Up

This hands-on walkthrough introduced the core steps involved in applying logistic regression Starting with data entry and ensuring the target variable is correctly formatted, we then visualized the relationship between the predictor and outcome, built a logistic model, and interpreted its output. We used the model to predict probabilities, translated those into class labels, and evaluated its accuracy with a confusion matrix.

Exercises

Logistic Regression

This exercise applies logistic regression in R to explore how numerical variables can be used to predict a binary outcome.

Dataset 1: Study Hours and Exam Results

This dataset helps determine whether the number of hours studied can predict whether a student passes an exam.

```
R Code
# Dataset 1
exam_data <- data.frame(
  Hours_Studied = c(1, 2, 3, 5, 4, 6, 7, 8, 2, 3, 9, 10),
  Passed_Binary = c(0, 0, 0, 1, 0, 1, 1, 1, 0, 0, 1, 1)
)


# Convert target to factor
exam_data$Passed_Binary <- factor(exam_data$Passed_Binary,
      levels = c(0, 1), labels = c("No", "Yes"))
```

1. Create a boxplot showing study hours grouped by whether the student passed. What patterns or differences do you observe?

2. Build a logistic regression model to predict pass/fail using study hours. What R function do you use, and what are the model terms?

3. Show the model summary. What do the coefficients tell you about the relationship between hours studied and passing?

4. Predict the probability of passing and create predicted class labels us-

ing a 0.5 cutoff. How many students are predicted to pass?

5. Make a confusion matrix and calculate the model accuracy. What proportion of predictions were correct?

Dataset 2: Heart Disease and Health Indicators

This dataset explores whether age and cholesterol levels can help predict whether a person has heart disease.

```
R Code
# Dataset 2
heart_data <- data.frame(
  Age = c(45, 50, 38, 60, 55, 42, 36, 62, 48, 53),
  Cholesterol = c(
    210, 230, 180, 250, 240, 195,
    170, 260, 220, 225
  ),
  Disease = c(1, 1, 0, 1, 1, 0, 0, 1, 0, 1)
)

# Convert target to factor
heart_data$Disease <- factor(heart_data$Disease,
  levels = c(0, 1), labels = c("No", "Yes")
)
```

6. Create two boxplots: one for age and one for cholesterol, grouped by disease status. Do either of these variables appear to show group separation?

7. Build a logistic regression model using both age and cholesterol to predict heart disease. What formula do you use?

8. Show the model summary. Which variable seems to have a stronger relationship with disease presence?

9. Use the model to predict disease probability and predicted class labels with a 0.5 cutoff. How many people are predicted to have heart disease?

10. Create a confusion matrix and calculate the accuracy. Is this model more or less accurate than the one from Dataset 1?

Lab 9

Decision Trees

In this lab, we explore how to build and interpret decision tree models. Decision trees are a method of classification that results in a visual display of how classification (not clustering) divides the data. By training a decision tree classifier on data, we have a tool for classifying new data.

Lesson Steps

Step 1: Load Required Packages

Before we can use decision trees and visualize them, we need that the required packages are installed and loaded. In this step, we check if the packages rpart and rpart.plot are available, install them if they are not, and then load them.

```
R Code
install.packages("rpart")
install.packages("rpart.plot")

library(rpart)
library(rpart.plot)
```

Step 2: Generate the Dataset

We created a sample dataset with 100 properties—half condos and half houses. The prices and square footage for each type were generated using different normal distributions: condos average around 250,000 dollars with about 1,200 square feet, while houses average around 600,000 dollars with roughly 2,500 square feet. To keep the results consistent across runs, we used a fixed random seed. The final dataset includes a categorical variable for property type, making it suitable for classification models like decision trees.

```
R Code

set.seed(42)
n <- 100

# Generate 50 condo listings
condos <- data.frame(
  price = round(rnorm(n / 2, mean = 250, sd = 40)),
  sf = round(rnorm(n / 2, mean = 1200, sd = 200)),
  type = "condo"
)

# Generate 50 house listings
houses <- data.frame(
  price = round(rnorm(n / 2, mean = 600, sd = 100)),
  sf = round(rnorm(n / 2, mean = 2500, sd = 400)),
  type = "house"
)

# Combine both into one dataset
df <- rbind(condos, houses)

# Convert 'type' to a factor for classification use
df$type <- factor(df$type)
```

Step 3: Visualize the Data

Before building a classification model, we want to make sure the data actually lends itself to classification. That means checking whether the properties naturally fall into groups based on at least one variable. If there's no real separation, a classification model wouldn't make much sense.

A good starting point is a scatter plot showing square footage versus price, with each point colored by property type. This helps us see whether condos and houses form distinct groups. In this context, "feature space" just means a plot where each axis represents a variable—like price or size—and each property is a point. If condos and houses cluster in different parts of the plot, it's a good sign that the model can learn to tell them apart.

```
R Code
# Labelled scatter plot

plot(df$sf, df$price,
  col = ifelse(df$type == "house",
    "#3D5A80", "#EE6C4D"
  ),
  pch = 19, xlab = "Square Footage", ylab = "Price",
  main = "Simulated Data: Price vs SF by Type"
)

legend("topright",
  legend = levels(df$type),
  col = c("#EE6C4D", "#3D5A80"), pch = 19
)
```

Simulated Data: Price vs SF by Type

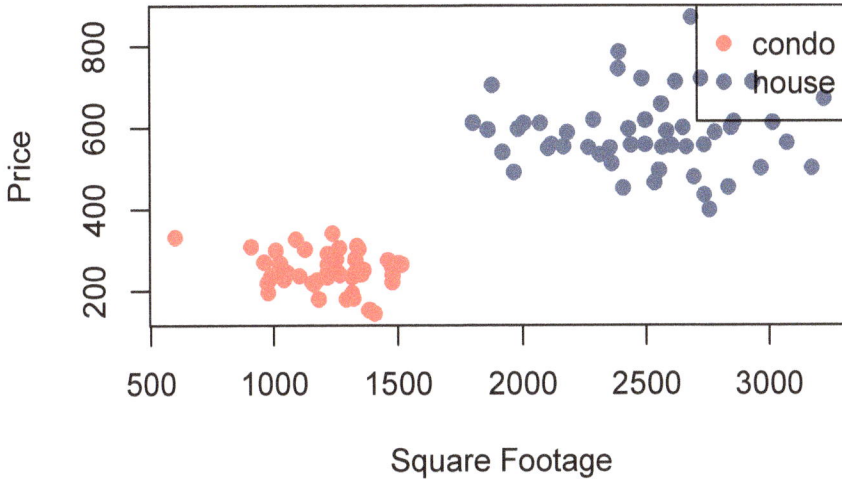

The scatterplot shows that houses tend to have higher square footage and price, which will help the decision tree learn to distinguish between them.

Step 4: Split the Dataset

To train and evaluate a model properly, we split the data into a training set and a test set. The training set will be used to build the model, and the test set will be used to check how well it performs on new data. This code will randomly select 80% of the data for training and the remaining 20% for testing and evaluating model performance. This is a fairly standard percentage split.

```
R Code
# Split to test and train
set.seed(123)
train_idx <- sample(seq_len(nrow(df)), size = 0.8 * nrow(df))
train_data <- df[train_idx, ]
test_data <- df[-train_idx, ]
```

Step 5: Train the Decision Tree

The decision tree (model) will be built using the training data. The tree will try to predict the type of property (house or condo) using the price and square footage as inputs. This line creates a classification tree with type as the target variable of house v condo and price and sf as predictor variables.

```
R Code
# Build tree model on training data
tree_model <- rpart(type ~ price + sf,
                    data = train_data, method = "class")
```

The output is stored in tree_model but to understand it we need a visualization.

Step 6: Plot the Decision Tree

Next, we visualize the trained decision tree in order to understand the tree model output. This plot shows the splits the tree makes based on the input features to classify the data.

R Code

```
# Tree model
rpart.plot(tree_model,
          main = "Decision Tree for Property Type")
```

Decision Tree for Property Type

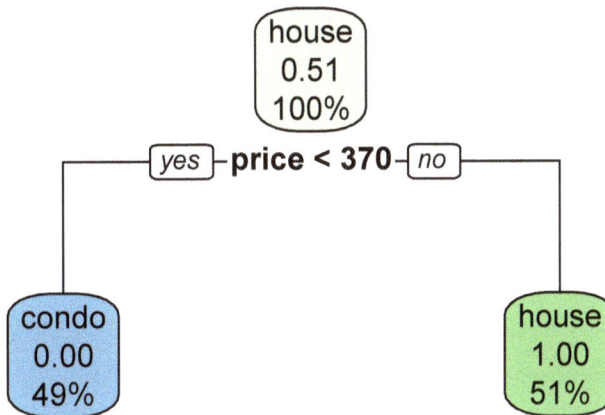

The resulting plot helps you understand how the tree is deciding between "house" and "condo" based on different thresholds of price and square footage. For this instance the criteria used is price. If price is below 370 then the decision tree is classifying it as a condo. If not it is considered a hosue.

Step 7: Predict and Evaluate the Model

Finally, we apply the decision tree model to the test data to see how well it performs. We compare the model's predictions to the actual property types and generate a confusion matrix.

```
R Code
# Evaluate
pred <- predict(tree_model, test_data, type = "class")
conf_matrix <- table(Predicted = pred,
                     Actual = test_data$type)
print(conf_matrix)
```

```
Output
##           Actual
## Predicted condo house
##     condo    11     0
##     house     0     9
```

The confusion matrix shows how many properties were correctly or incorrectly classified. This gives a basic sense of model accuracy and can highlight areas where the model may be making errors. In this case there are no misclassifications.

Wrap-up

This lab demonstrates how decision trees use feature thresholds to classify observations effectively. The clear separation between condos and houses in price and size helps the model achieve accurate predictions, as confirmed by the confusion matrix. Understanding this process provides a solid foundation for applying decision trees to other classification problems in practice.

Exercises

Decision Trees

In these exercises you will build and evaluate a decision tree model to classify. Start by generating a synthetic dataset. Then we visualize the data, split it into training and test sets, train a decision tree model, and finally assess its performance using a confusion matrix.

Dataset 1: Customer Churn Prediction

```
R Code
set.seed(55)
m <- 120

# Generate customers who did not churn
no_churn <- data.frame(
  monthly_charges = round(rnorm(m / 2, mean = 50, sd = 10)),
  tenure_months = round(rnorm(m / 2, mean = 30, sd = 12)),
  churn = "No"
)


# Generate customers who churned
churn <- data.frame(
  monthly_charges = round(rnorm(m / 2, mean = 75, sd = 15)),
  tenure_months = round(rnorm(m / 2, mean = 8, sd = 5)),
  churn = "Yes"
)


# Combine and factorize churn variable
customer_data <- rbind(no_churn, churn)
customer_data$churn <- factor(customer_data$churn)
```

1. Plot monthly charges versus tenure in months, coloring points by churn status. What trends do you notice between the groups?
2. Split the dataset into 70% training and 30% testing sets using a random seed of 202. Show the code and number of rows in each set.
3. Build a decision tree model predicting churn from monthly charges and tenure using the training data. Which function and parameters do you use?
4. Visualize the decision tree. What variable and threshold does the first split use?
5. Predict churn status on the test set and generate a confusion matrix. How many customers were misclassified?

Dataset 2: Loans

Here is a second dataset of customer loan applications with two features — income and loan amount — and a binary outcome of loan approval.

R Code
```
set.seed(101)
m <- 120

approved <- data.frame(
  income = round(rnorm(m / 2, mean = 70, sd = 15)),
  loan_amount = round(rnorm(m / 2, mean = 10, sd = 5)),
  approved = "Yes"
)

denied <- data.frame(
  income = round(rnorm(m / 2, mean = 45, sd = 10)),
  loan_amount = round(rnorm(m / 2, mean = 20, sd = 7)),
  approved = "No"
)

loan_data <- rbind(approved, denied)
loan_data$approved <- factor(loan_data$approved)
```

6. Plot loan amount versus income colored by loan approval status. What can you infer about the separation between approved and denied applicants?

7. Split the data into 75% training and 25% test sets with seed 202. Show the size of each set.

8. Train a decision tree to predict approval status from income and loan amount on the training set. Provide the code used.

9. Plot the resulting decision tree. What is the primary factor the model uses to decide approval?

10. Predict approval on the test set and create a confusion matrix. How accurate is the model?

Lab 10

K-Nearest Neighbors Classification

The k-Nearest Neighbors (kNN) algorithm is a simple classification method used to predict the category of a data point based on similarity (mathematical distance based) to known examples. It works by comparing a test observation to its nearest neighbors in the training data using a distance measure, typically Euclidean distance.

In this lab, we walk through the entire kNN classification process— from preparing and normalizing the data to training the model, making predictions, and evaluating results.

Lesson Steps

Step 1: Load Required Libraries

Before starting any data analysis in R we need to load the necessary libraries. The `class` package provides the `knn()` function to run the k-Nearest Neighbors classification algorithm. The `ggplot2` package is used to create clear and informative visualizations of the data and model predictions.

R Code
```
# Install if not already installed
options(repos = c(CRAN = "https://cran.r-project.org"))
install.packages("class")
install.packages("ggplot2")


library(class)
library(ggplot2)
```

Step 2: Load the Data

We create here a sample dataset, which contains measurements of height, weight, and corresponding pant size for a group of 30 people.

R Code

```
pants_data <- data.frame(
  Height = c(
    158, 158, 158, 160, 160, 163, 163,
    160, 163, 165, 161, 163, 163,
    160, 163, 165, 165, 168, 168, 168,
    171, 170, 170, 160, 160, 163, 163,
    160, 163, 165
  ),
  Weight = c(
    58, 59, 63, 59, 60, 60, 61, 64, 64, 61,
    60, 62, 61, 63, 64, 62, 65, 62, 63, 66,
    63, 64, 68, 58, 60, 60, 61, 64, 63, 61
  ),
  PantSize = c(
    "M", "M", "M", "M", "M", "M", "M",
    "L", "L", "L", "M", "M", "M",
    "L", "L", "L", "L", "L", "L", "L",
    "L", "L", "L", "M", "M", "M", "M",
    "L", "L", "L"
  )
)

head(pants_data)
```

```
Output
##     Height Weight PantSize
## 1     158     58       M
## 2     158     59       M
## 3     158     63       M
## 4     160     59       M
## 5     160     60       M
## 6     163     60       M
```

Step 3: Convert Pant Size to a Factor

To indicate that pant size is a categorical variable (with categories "M" and "L"), we convert the PantSize column into a factor. This is important because the kNN algorithm treats factor variables as categories to classify.

```
R Code
# Convert PantSize to factor (categorical)
pants_data$PantSize <- as.factor(pants_data$PantSize)
```

Step 4: Normalize Numeric Variables

kNN uses distance to identify nearest neighbors, so features (input variables) must be on a similar scale. Here, we define a function normalize() to perform z-score normalization (subtract the mean and divide by the standard deviation). Then we apply this normalization to both height and weight columns, creating new normalized columns. We do not want to normalize the entire data frame since some of the variables are not numeric.

R Code
```
# Normalize
normalize <- function(x) {
  (x - mean(x)) / sd(x)
}


pants_data$Height_norm <- normalize(pants_data$Height)
pants_data$Weight_norm <- normalize(pants_data$Weight)


head(pants_data)
```

Output

##	Height	Weight	PantSize	Height_norm	Weight_norm
## 1	158	58	M	-1.42094942	-1.6836691
## 2	158	59	M	-1.42094942	-1.2592147
## 3	158	63	M	-1.42094942	0.4386029
## 4	160	59	M	-0.87791142	-1.2592147
## 5	160	60	M	-0.87791142	-0.8347603
## 6	163	60	M	-0.06335443	-0.8347603

Step 5: Split Data into Training and Testing Sets

So we can evaluate the model later, we need to split the dataset randomly into training and testing sets, using 80% of the data for training and 20% for testing. We set a random seed for reproducibility so that the split remains the same each time the code is run.

```
R Code
# Split into train and test
set.seed(123)   # For reproducibility
sample_indices <- sample(1:nrow(pants_data),
                      size = 0.8 * nrow(pants_data))


train_data <- pants_data[sample_indices, ]
test_data <- pants_data[-sample_indices, ]
```

Step 6: Prepare Features and Labels for Model Training and Testing

Before we can train a k-nearest neighbors (kNN) model, we need to split the data into two parts: the input features and the target labels. The features are the numerical values the model uses to compare individuals—in this case, height and weight, which we normalize first. We pull these features separately for both the training and test sets. The labels are what we want the model to predict—pant size, like M or L—and we only use the labels from the training set so the model can learn the connection between body size and pant size. This setup lets the kNN algorithm look at a new case, find the most similar examples from the training set, and predict based on those.

R Code
```
# Prep data
train_features <- train_data[, c(
  "Height_norm",
  "Weight_norm"
)]
test_features <- test_data[, c(
  "Height_norm",
  "Weight_norm"
)]
train_labels <- train_data$PantSize


head(train_features)
```

Output
```
##     Height_norm Weight_norm
## 15 -0.06335443  0.86305725
## 19  1.29424055  0.43860286
## 14 -0.87791142  0.43860286
## 3  -1.42094942  0.43860286
## 10  0.47968356 -0.41030590
## 18  1.29424055  0.01414848
```

R Code
```
head(test_features)
```

Output
```
##     Height_norm Weight_norm
## 2   -1.42094942 -1.25921467
## 6   -0.06335443 -0.83476029
## 12  -0.06335443  0.01414848
## 13  -0.06335443 -0.41030590
## 16   0.47968356  0.01414848
## 29  -0.06335443  0.43860286
```

R Code
```
head(train_labels)
```

Output
```
## [1] L L L M L L
## Levels: L M
```

The result is below (the number on the left is the row of the original data).

Step 7: Run kNN Classification with k = 3

In k-nearest neighbors (kNN), k is a number that tells the algorithm how many nearby data points (neighbors) it should look at when making a prediction. For example, if k = 3, the model will find the three closest points to a new data point and predict the label (like pant size) based on the majority vote from those three neighbors. So, k controls how many comparisons the model makes to decide what category the new data belongs to.

Choosing k = 3 in k-nearest neighbors (kNN) is common because it offers a simple, balanced starting point. If you set k = 1, the prediction depends only on the closest neighbor, which makes the model very sensitive to noise or unusual points. On the other hand, if k is too large (like 10), the model may include too many faraway points that don't really match the test case, which can blur the differences between categories. Using k = 3 gives a nice middle ground — it reduces the risk of random errors from one data point while still focusing on the local pattern. It's not the perfect value for every case, but it's often a good place to start. The value used for k is always odd since an even k would result in ties.

Now we perform kNN classification with k = 3, meaning that the algorithm will look at the 3 nearest neighbors of each test point to decide its pant size, using majority voting among those neighbors.

```
R Code
# Run kNN


k3 <- 3
pred_test_k3 <- knn(
  train = train_features,
  test = test_features, cl = train_labels, k = k3
)
```

The result shows the predicted pant sizes for each observation in your test dataset (which has 20% of the data original size 30 so 6 test data) after running the k-Nearest Neighbors (kNN) classification with k = 3.

Step 8: Evaluate the k=3 Model

We compare the predicted pant sizes with the actual sizes in the test set by printing a confusion matrix. This matrix shows how many points were correctly classified and where the model made mistakes.

R Code
```
# Evaluate the model


cat("Confusion matrix for k=3:\n")
```

Output
```
## Confusion matrix for k=3:
```

R Code
```
print(table(
  Predicted = pred_test_k3,
  Actual = test_data$PantSize
))
```

Output
```
##          Actual
## Predicted L M
##        L  1 0
##        M  1 4
```

The result of the classification is below. One sample is misclassified.

Step 9: Plotting the Result

A scatterplot code can visualize the kNN test results, using ggplot2.

R Code

```
# Add predictions to test data for plotting
test_data$Predicted <- pred_test_k3


# Plot: test points only
test_data$Predicted <- as.character(pred_test_k3)


ggplot(test_data, aes(
  x = Height, y = Weight,
  color = Predicted, shape = PantSize
)) +
  geom_point(size = 4) +
  labs(
    title = "kNN Test Predictions (k=3)",
    x = "Height",
    y = "Weight",
    color = "Predicted Size",
    shape = "Actual Size"
  ) +
  theme_minimal()
```

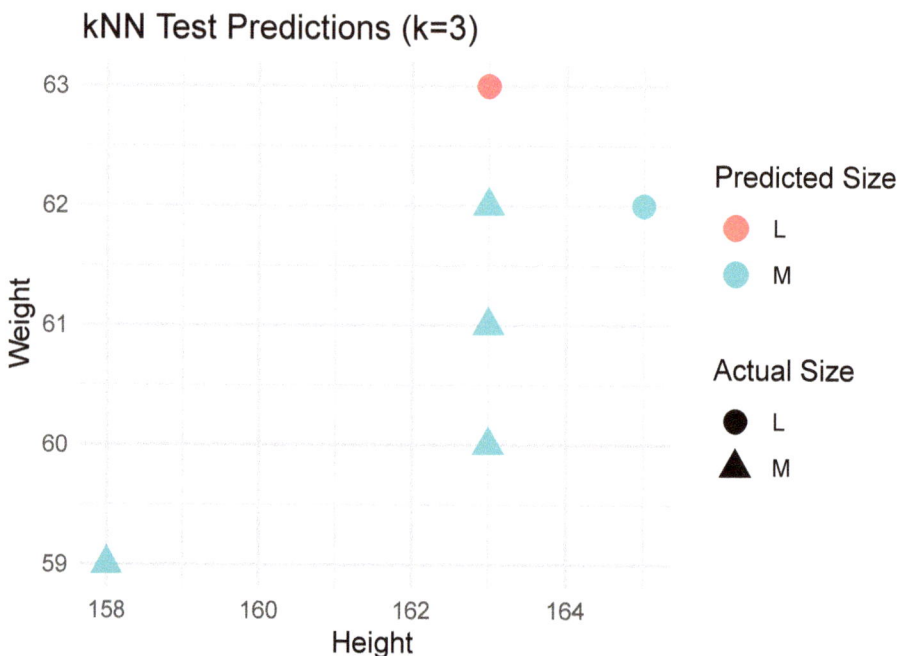

kNN Test Predictions (k=3)

The plot shows the test data points, colored by the predicted pant size, and shapes for the actual pant size so you can visually compare:

Wrap-Up

Through this example, we can see how kNN uses distance-based comparisons to make classifications and how factors like normalization and choice of k affect performance. Even with a small dataset, the process highlights the practical considerations in building and testing a classification model—especially the importance of careful data preparation and evaluation. The methods learned here serve as a foundation for applying kNN to more complex, real-world problems in machine learning and predictive analytics.

Exercises

K Nearest Neighbor

Dataset 1: Shoe Size Prediction

You are given measurements of foot length and foot width for 30 individuals, along with their shoe size category:

S (Small)

M (Medium)

L (Large)

The goal is to classify shoe size based on foot dimensions.

```
R Code
shoe_data <- data.frame(
  FootLength = c(22.5, 23.0, 23.2, 23.5, 23.7,
                 24.0, 24.3, 24.5, 24.7, 25.0,
                 25.2, 25.5, 25.8, 26.0, 26.3,
                 26.5, 26.8, 27.0, 27.3, 27.5,
                 27.8, 28.0, 28.3, 28.5, 28.7,
                 29.0, 29.2, 29.5, 29.8, 30.0),
  FootWidth = c(8.0, 8.2, 8.1, 8.4, 8.3, 8.5, 8.6,
             8.7, 8.8, 8.9, 9.0, 9.1, 9.0, 9.2,
             9.3, 9.4, 9.5, 9.6, 9.6, 9.7,
             9.8, 9.9, 9.9, 10.0, 10.1, 10.1,
             10.2, 10.3, 10.3, 10.4),
  ShoeSize = c("S", "S", "S", "S", "S", "S", "S",
             "M", "M", "M", "M", "M", "M", "M",
             "M", "M", "L", "L", "L", "L",
             "L", "L", "L", "L", "L", "L",
             "L", "L", "L", "L")
)
```

1. What are the first 5 rows of the `shoe_data` dataset?

2. After converting `ShoeSize` to a factor, what does the output of `str(shoe_data)` show?

3. Normalize `FootLength` and `FootWidth`. What are the mean and standard deviation of each column before normalization?

4. How many rows are in the training and test sets after using an 80/20 split?

5. What do the first 3 rows of the training features look like?

6. What are the corresponding labels of the training features?

7. What are the predicted shoe sizes for the test set using k = 3?

8. How many test set predictions were correctly classified?

9. What does the confusion matrix show?

10. After creating the scatterplot, are there any misclassifications you can visually identify?

Dataset 2: Fruit Type

This dataset includes chemical properties (sugar and acidity levels) of 30 fruits. The goal is to classify what kind of fruit.

R Code

```
fruit_data <- data.frame(
  Sugar = c(
    10.2, 10.5, 10.3, 10.8, 10.6, 11.0,
    11.2, 11.5, 11.3, 11.8,
    12.0, 12.2, 12.5, 12.3, 12.8, 13.0,
    13.2, 13.5, 13.3, 13.7,
    14.0, 14.2, 14.5, 14.3, 14.7, 14.9,
    15.0, 15.2, 15.5, 15.3
  ),
  Acidity = c(
    3.5, 3.4, 3.6, 3.7, 3.6, 3.8, 3.9,
    4.0, 4.1, 4.0, 4.2, 4.3, 4.4, 4.5,
    4.4, 4.6, 4.7, 4.6, 4.8, 4.9,
    5.0, 5.1, 5.0, 5.2, 5.3, 5.4, 5.5,
    5.4, 5.6, 5.7
  ),
  FruitType = c(
    "Apple", "Apple", "Apple", "Apple",
    "Apple", "Apple", "Apple", "Orange",
    "Orange", "Orange",
    "Orange", "Orange", "Orange", "Orange",
    "Orange", "Banana", "Banana", "Banana",
    "Banana", "Banana", "Banana", "Banana",
    "Banana", "Banana", "Banana", "Banana",
    "Banana", "Banana", "Banana", "Banana"
  )
)
```

11. What does the first 5 rows of `fruit_data` look like?

12. After converting `FruitType` to a factor, how many levels does it have?

13. Normalize `Sugar` and `Acidity`. What are their means and standard deviations before normalization?

14. After splitting the dataset into training and testing sets, how many observations are in each?

15. What are the column names of your feature set?

16. What do the first 2 training labels look like?

17. What are the predicted labels for the test set using k = 3?

18. Did the model confuse any fruit types?

19. How many predictions were accurate?

20. What does the confusion matrix indicate?

21. After plotting predictions, what insights can you draw from the placement and accuracy of points?

Lab 11

Simple Association Analysis

Association analysis is an important technique in market basket analysis that helps identify relationships between items in transactional data. By studying how frequently items are purchased together, businesses can uncover patterns that inform product placement, promotions, and personalized recommendations. In this lab, we explore the basic concepts of support, confidence, and lift. Through step-by-step calculations, we develop an intuitive understanding of how item relationships can be quantified and interpreted.

Lesson Steps

Step 1: Set up a Simple Dataset

First let's create a small dataset of market basket transactions manually. Each transaction is a list of items bought by a customer. This dataset will be stored as a list object where each list member is an individual transaction (for example transaction 1, list member 1, is the items purchased of apple and banana).

R Code

```
# Step 1: Create a list of transactions manually
transactions <- list(
  c("apple", "banana"),
  c("banana", "orange"),
  c("apple", "orange"),
  c("apple", "banana", "orange"),
  c("banana")
)


# View the transactions
print(transactions)
```

Output

```
## [[1]]
## [1] "apple"  "banana"
##
## [[2]]
## [1] "banana" "orange"
##
## [[3]]
## [1] "apple"  "orange"
##
## [[4]]
## [1] "apple"  "banana" "orange"
##
## [[5]]
## [1] "banana"
```

This list represents five shopping baskets, with each element corresponding to a different customer's basket. It introduces several key concepts used in market basket analysis. A transaction refers to a single list of items purchased together by one customer. An item is an individual product, such as "apple." An itemset is a combination of one or more items, such as {apple, banana}, indicating the grouping of products that may be bought together.

Step 2: Manually Count Frequencies (Support)

Next let's count how many times items or itemsets appear in the dataset.

```
R Code
# Count how many times each item appears
item_counts <- table(unlist(transactions))
print(item_counts)
```

```
Output
##
##   apple banana orange
##       3      4      3
```

This gives a simple frequency of how many transactions contain the grocery item not accounting for what other items were purchased in the same transaction.

It is insightful to know the proportion of transactions that contain a certain item. For example, if 100 transactions are made in a store and 30 of these purchase milk then the proportion of transactions containing milk is 0.3. This metric is called support, and it measures the proportion of transactions that contain a specific item (or itemset). Support helps us understand how common or popular an item (or itemset) is in the dataset.

```
R Code
# Calculate support manually
total_t <- length(transactions)
support_apple <- item_counts["apple"] / total_t
support_banana <- item_counts["banana"] / total_t
support_orange <- item_counts["orange"] / total_t

cat("Support for apple:", support_apple, "\n")
```

```
Output
## Support for apple: 0.6
```

```
R Code
cat("Support for banana:", support_banana, "\n")
```

```
Output
## Support for banana: 0.8
```

```
R Code
cat("Support for orange:", support_orange, "\n")
```

```
Output
## Support for orange: 0.6
```

The results – such as the support for apple being 0.6 – are what would be expected (for the 5 transactions in the list, 3 have apples, thus 0.6 is the support).

Step 3: Count Joint Itemset (2-item support)

In step 2 we only considered individual items however often considering itemsets (with 2 or more items) is important because it helps uncover patterns in customer buying behavior—specifically, which pairs of products are frequently purchased together. This insight is the foundation for market basket analysis. Applications of this in business include: product placement decisions (e.g., placing commonly paired items near each other in a store), create bundle deals or promotions (e.g., discounts on items often bought together) or build recommendation systems (e.g., "Customers who bought this also bought...").

By identifying frequent item pairs, we can later move on to generate association rules, which describe the likelihood of buying one item when another is already in the basket. This step ensures we're only focusing on meaningful combinations with enough support to be useful.

Let's consider the two-item itemset case of apple and banana.

R Code
```
# Define function to check if a set of items
# is in a transaction
has_items <- function(transaction, items) {
  all(items %in% transaction)
}


# Count how many times apple and banana appear together
count_apple_banana <- sum(sapply(transactions,
  has_items,
  items = c("apple", "banana")
))
support_apple_banana <- count_apple_banana / total_t

cat(
  "Support for {apple, banana}:",
  support_apple_banana, "\n"
)
```

Output
```
## Support for {apple, banana}: 0.4
```

The result shows the support for the itemset of apple and banana (2-item itemset) is 0.4. Going back to the original transaction list in 2 of the 5 transactions there is both apple and banana purchased so this result makes sense.

Step 4: Calculate Confidence

Confidence tells us how likely it is that someone will buy one item if they have already bought another. Note this case like conditional probability it is based on - order matters, first bread then butter is different from first butter then bread. For example, if many people who buy bread also buy butter, the confidence of the rule "bread → butter" is high. It is calculated by dividing the number of times both items are bought together by the number of times the first item is bought. Confidence helps us find strong and useful shopping patterns, so stores can decide which items to recommend or put together in a sale.

Let's use confidence to measure how likely banana is bought if apple is bought.

R Code
```
# Confidence for apple → banana = P(banana | apple)
count_apple <- sum(sapply(transactions, has_items,
  items = c("apple")
))
confidence_aTob <- count_apple_banana / count_apple
cat(
  "Confidence for apple → banana:", confidence_aTob,
  "\n"
)
```

Output
```
## Confidence for apple → banana: 0.6666667
```

The interpretation of the results for confidence for apple → banana is that

2/3 (0.6666...) of customers who bought apples also bought bananas. This is confirmed by looking back at the original data where of 5 transactions 3 bought apples. The three is the denominator of the confidence calculation and since we see that 2 of the three also bought bananas this gives the correct confidence ratio.

Step 5: Calculate Lift

The third and final association metric is called lift. Lift is a measure used to understand how much more likely two items are to be bought together compared to if they were bought independently. It helps us see whether an association between items is meaningful or just due to chance. Lift is calculated by dividing the confidence of the rule (for example, apple → banana) by the overall support of the second item (banana).

If the lift is greater than 1, it means the items are more likely to be bought together than expected, showing a positive association. A lift equal to 1 means the items are bought together exactly as often as expected by chance, indicating no real association. A lift less than 1 means the items are less likely to be bought together than expected.

```
R Code
# P(banana)
support_ban <- item_counts["banana"] / total_t

# Lift = confidence / support of consequent
lift_apple_to_banana <- confidence_aTob / support_ban
cat("Lift for apple → banana:", lift_apple_to_banana,
    "\n")
```

Output
```
## Lift for apple → banana: 0.8333333
```

From above the confidence for apple → banana is 2/3 and the support for banana is 8/10 (0.8) so the lift for apple → banana is 2/3 divided by 8/10 which is 5/6 or 0.8333... as the result below shows.

This means that buying apples actually makes it slightly less likely that someone will buy bananas, compared to the average shopper. Because the lift is less than 1, there is no strong association, and in fact, the items are bought together less than expected by chance.

If for example, if the confidence of apple → banana were 0.6 and the support of banana were 0.3, then the lift is 2.0. This means people who buy apples are twice as likely to buy bananas compared to random shoppers, showing a strong connection between the two items.

Wrap-Up

This simple example provides a clear foundation for understanding how association analysis works in practice. By calculating support, confidence, and lift, we gain insight into how items interact within transactions and how to assess the strength and direction of those interactions. These principles can now be scaled up to larger datasets and more complex itemsets to guide business strategy and enhance customer experience through data-driven decision making.

Lab 11 Exercises

Basic Association Analysis

This exercise set includes two datasets for practicing association analysis concepts such as support, confidence, and lift.

Dataset 1: Grocery Transactions

```
R Code
transactions2 <- list(
  c("milk", "bread"),
  c("bread", "butter"),
  c("milk", "butter"),
  c("milk", "bread", "butter"),
  c("bread")
)
```

1. How many transactions are there in this dataset?

2. Count the frequency of each individual item: milk, bread, and butter.

3. Calculate the support for each item.

4. Calculate the support for the two-item itemsets: {milk, bread}, {bread, butter}, {milk, butter}.

5. Calculate the confidence of the rule: milk → butter.

6. Calculate the confidence of the rule: bread → butter.

7. Calculate the lift of the rule: milk → butter.

8. Interpret the lift for the rule milk → butter. What does it tell you about the relationship between these two items?

Dataset 2: Coffee Shop Orders

```
R Code
transactions3 <- list(
  c("coffee", "donut"),
  c("coffee", "sandwich"),
  c("tea", "donut"),
  c("coffee", "donut", "sandwich"),
  c("tea"),
  c("coffee", "sandwich"),
  c("donut")
)
```

9. How many transactions are there in this dataset?
10. Count the number of times each item (coffee, tea, donut, sandwich) appears.
11. Calculate the support for each individual item.
12. Calculate the support for the following two-item itemsets:

   - {coffee, donut}
   - {coffee, sandwich}
   - {tea, donut}

13. Calculate the confidence for the rule: coffee → donut.
14. Calculate the confidence for the rule: donut → coffee.
15. Calculate the lift for the rule: coffee → donut.
16. Based on the lift, what can you conclude about the association between coffee and donut?
17. Which item has the highest support and what does that indicate about customer preferences?

Lab 12

Association Analysis using Package arules

Introduction

This lab builds on the previous hand-coded example from Lab 11 and introduces the powerful R package arules for association rule mining. Using this package is scalable for larger datasets and provides professional tools for mining frequent itemsets and association rules.

Lesson Steps

Step 1: Install and Load Required Packages

The **arules** package provides tools for mining association rules and frequent itemsets, primarily used in market basket analysis.

R Code
```
# Install if not already installed
options(repos = c(CRAN = "https://cran.r-project.org"))
# Install if needed
install.packages("arules")


# Load the package
library(arules)
```

Step 2: Create the Transactions Object

A transactions object in arules represents transactional data in a specialized sparse matrix format, optimized for mining frequent itemsets and rules.

Here we recreate the small example from the previous lab as a list, then convert it into a transactions object.

```
R Code
# Manually create a list of transactions
raw_transactions <- list(
  c("apple", "banana"),
  c("banana", "orange"),
  c("apple", "orange"),
  c("apple", "banana", "orange"),
  c("banana")
)


# Convert to transactions object
trans <- as(raw_transactions, "transactions")


# View a summary
summary(trans)
```

Output

```
## transactions as itemMatrix in sparse format with
##  5 rows (elements/itemsets/transactions) and
##  3 columns (items) and a density of 0.6666667
##
## most frequent items:
##  banana    apple  orange (Other)
##       4        3        3       0
##
## element (itemset/transaction) length distribution:
## sizes
## 1 2 3
## 1 3 1
##
##     Min. 1st Qu.  Median    Mean 3rd Qu.    Max.
##        1       2       2       2       2       3
##
## includes extended item information - examples:
##    labels
## 1  apple
## 2 banana
## 3 orange
```

The output summary describes the number of transactions, items, density, and frequency distributions.

R Code

```
# Inspect actual transactions
inspect(trans)
```

Output
```
##      items
## [1] {apple, banana}
## [2] {banana, orange}
## [3] {apple, orange}
## [4] {apple, banana, orange}
## [5] {banana}
```

This shows the individual items in each transaction.

Step 3: Item Frequency and Support

You can visualize item frequencies using `itemFrequencyPlot()`.

R Code
```
itemFrequencyPlot(trans, topN = 10, type = "absolute",
                  col = "#637D8D")
```

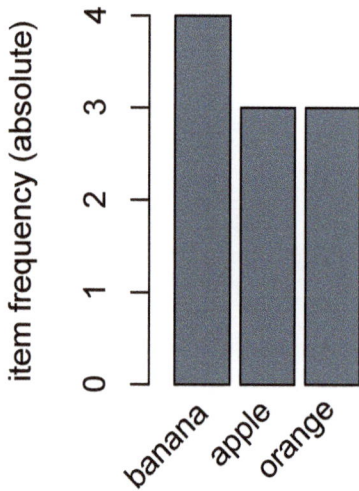

Get support values (relative frequency) of each item:

```
R Code
itemFrequency(trans)
```

```
Output
##    apple banana orange
##     0.6    0.8    0.6
```

Step 4: Generate Association Rules

Use the Apriori algorithm to find rules with minimum support and confidence thresholds.

R Code
```
rules <- apriori(trans,
  parameter = list(supp = 0.2, conf = 0.5))
```

This finds rules where the itemsets occur in at least 20% of transactions and rules have at least 50% confidence.

Step 5: Inspect the Rules

View the rules generated:

R Code
```
for (i in 1:length(rules)) {
  cat(
    "[", i, "] ", labels(lhs(rules[i])), "=>",
    labels(rhs(rules[i])),
    " | lift:", round(quality(rules[i])$lift, 3),
    "\n"
  )
}
```

Output

```
## [ 1 ]  {} => {apple}  | lift: 1
## [ 2 ]  {} => {orange}  | lift: 1
## [ 3 ]  {} => {banana}  | lift: 1
## [ 4 ]  {apple} => {orange}  | lift: 1.111
## [ 5 ]  {orange} => {apple}  | lift: 1.111
## [ 6 ]  {apple} => {banana}  | lift: 0.833
## [ 7 ]  {banana} => {apple}  | lift: 0.833
## [ 8 ]  {orange} => {banana}  | lift: 0.833
## [ 9 ]  {banana} => {orange}  | lift: 0.833
## [ 10 ]  {apple,orange} => {banana}  | lift: 0.625
## [ 11 ]  {apple,banana} => {orange}  | lift: 0.833
## [ 12 ]  {banana,orange} => {apple}  | lift: 0.833
```

R Code

```r
for (i in 1:length(rules)) {
  cat(
    "[", i, "] ",
    labels(lhs(rules[i])), " => ",
    labels(rhs(rules[i])),
    " | confidence: ",
    round(quality(rules[i])$confidence, 3),
    "\n"
  )
}
```

Output

```
## [ 1 ]   {}  =>  {apple}   | confidence:   0.6
## [ 2 ]   {}  =>  {orange}  | confidence:   0.6
## [ 3 ]   {}  =>  {banana}  | confidence:   0.8
## [ 4 ]   {apple}  =>  {orange}  | confidence:   0.667
## [ 5 ]   {orange}  =>  {apple}  | confidence:   0.667
## [ 6 ]   {apple}  =>  {banana}  | confidence:   0.667
## [ 7 ]   {banana}  =>  {apple}  | confidence:   0.5
## [ 8 ]   {orange}  =>  {banana}  | confidence:   0.667
## [ 9 ]   {banana}  =>  {orange}  | confidence:   0.5
## [ 10 ]   {apple,orange}  =>  {banana}  | confidence:   0.5
## [ 11 ]   {apple,banana}  =>  {orange}  | confidence:   0.5
## [ 12 ]   {banana,orange}  =>  {apple}  | confidence:   0.5
```

R Code

```r
for (i in 1:length(rules)) {
  cat(
    "[", i, "] ",
    labels(lhs(rules[i])), " => ",
    labels(rhs(rules[i])),
    " | support: ", round(quality(rules[i])$support, 3),
    "\n"
  )
}
```

Output

```
## [ 1 ]  {}  =>  {apple}   | support:   0.6
## [ 2 ]  {}  =>  {orange}  | support:   0.6
## [ 3 ]  {}  =>  {banana}  | support:   0.8
## [ 4 ]  {apple}  =>  {orange}  | support:   0.4
## [ 5 ]  {orange}  =>  {apple}  | support:   0.4
## [ 6 ]  {apple}  =>  {banana}  | support:   0.4
## [ 7 ]  {banana}  =>  {apple}  | support:   0.4
## [ 8 ]  {orange}  =>  {banana}  | support:   0.4
## [ 9 ]  {banana}  =>  {orange}  | support:   0.4
## [ 10 ]  {apple,orange}  =>  {banana}  | support:   0.2
## [ 11 ]  {apple,banana}  =>  {orange}  | support:   0.2
## [ 12 ]  {banana,orange}  =>  {apple}  | support:   0.2
```

Sort rules by lift to find the strongest associations:

R Code

```r
sorted_rules <- sort(rules, by = "lift")

for (i in seq_along(sorted_rules)) {
  lhs_str <- labels(lhs(sorted_rules[i]))
  rhs_str <- labels(rhs(sorted_rules[i]))
  lift_val <- round(quality(sorted_rules[i])$lift, 3)

  cat(
    "[", i, "] ", lhs_str, " => ", rhs_str,
    " | lift: ", lift_val, "\n"
  )
}
```

Output

```
## [ 1 ]   {apple}  =>  {orange}  | lift:  1.111
## [ 2 ]   {orange}  =>  {apple}  | lift:  1.111
## [ 3 ]   {}  =>  {apple}  | lift:  1
## [ 4 ]   {}  =>  {orange}  | lift:  1
## [ 5 ]   {}  =>  {banana}  | lift:  1
## [ 6 ]   {banana}  =>  {apple}  | lift:  0.833
## [ 7 ]   {banana}  =>  {orange}  | lift:  0.833
## [ 8 ]   {apple,banana}  =>  {orange}  | lift:  0.833
## [ 9 ]   {banana,orange}  =>  {apple}  | lift:  0.833
## [ 10 ]   {apple}  =>  {banana}  | lift:  0.833
## [ 11 ]   {orange}  =>  {banana}  | lift:  0.833
## [ 12 ]   {apple,orange}  =>  {banana}  | lift:  0.625
```

Step 6: Filter Specific Rule (e.g. apple → banana)

To focus on rules of interest, filter the rules for specific antecedents and consequents.

R Code

```
# Subset rules where apple is on the left-hand side
# and banana on the right-hand side

subset_rules <- subset(rules,
         lhs %in% "apple" & rhs %in% "banana")

# note using inspect() is easier but this is
# for print display

for (i in 1:length(subset_rules)) {
  cat(
    "[", i, "] ", labels(lhs(subset_rules[i])), "=>",
    labels(rhs(subset_rules[i])),
    " | lift:", round(quality(subset_rules[i])$lift, 3),
    "\n"
  )
}
```

Output

```
## [ 1 ]  {apple} => {banana}  | lift: 0.833
## [ 2 ]  {apple,orange} => {banana}  | lift: 0.625
```

R Code

```
for (i in 1:length(subset_rules)) {
  cat(
    "[", i, "] ",
    labels(lhs(subset_rules[i])), " => ",
    labels(rhs(subset_rules[i])),
    " | confidence: ",
    round(quality(subset_rules[i])$confidence, 3),
    "\n"
  )
}
```

Output

```
## [ 1 ]  {apple}  =>  {banana}  | confidence:  0.667
## [ 2 ]  {apple,orange}  =>  {banana}  | confidence:  0.5
```

R Code

```
for (i in 1:length(subset_rules)) {
  cat(
    "[", i, "] ",
    labels(lhs(subset_rules[i])), " => ",
    labels(rhs(subset_rules[i])),
    " | support: ",
    round(quality(subset_rules[i])$support, 3),
    "\n"
  )
}
```

```
Output
## [ 1 ]   {apple}  =>  {banana}  | support:  0.4
## [ 2 ]   {apple,orange}  =>  {banana}  | support:  0.2
```

Wrap-Up

This lab demonstrated how to use the arules package in R to efficiently per-form association rule mining. By converting transaction data into the proper format, visualizing item frequencies, and applying the Apriori algorithm, we were able to generate, inspect, and filter association rules based on sup-port, confidence, and lift. Compared to manually coded methods, the arules package streamlines the process and scales well for larger datasets. Under-standing how to interpret and refine these rules helps uncover meaningful patterns in categorical data—especially useful in applications like market basket analysis, recommendation systems, and customer behavior insights.

Exercises

Association Analysis using arules

In this exercise, you'll practice using the `arules` package in R to perform association rule mining.

Dataset 1: Bookstore Transactions**

The first dataset simulates book purchases at a small bookstore. Each transaction represents the set of books bought together by a customer.

```
R Code
#need to load library(arules)

# Create bookstore transactions
book_data <- list(
  c("fiction", "romance"),
  c("fiction", "mystery"),
  c("nonfiction", "history"),
  c("fiction", "mystery", "romance"),
  c("nonfiction", "selfhelp"),
  c("romance", "mystery"),
  c("fiction", "history"),
  c("romance", "selfhelp"),
  c("fiction", "nonfiction"),
  c("history", "selfhelp")
)

book_trans <- as(book_data, "transactions")
```

1. Show the output of `summary(book_trans)`. How many transactions

and unique items are there?

2. Use `inspect(book_trans)` and describe one transaction in words.

3. Plot the item frequency using `itemFrequencyPlot()`. What is the most frequent item?

4. Generate association rules with `supp = 0.2` and `conf = 0.5`. How many rules are generated?

5. Sort the rules by lift and inspect the top 3. Which rule has the highest lift and what does it mean?

Dataset 2: Coffee Shop Orders

The second dataset represents items customers often order together at a coffee shop.

```
R Code
# Create coffee shop transactions
coffee_data <- list(
  c("coffee", "bagel"),
  c("coffee", "donut"),
  c("tea", "cookie"),
  c("coffee", "cookie"),
  c("donut", "bagel"),
  c("tea", "bagel"),
  c("coffee", "tea"),
  c("bagel", "cookie"),
  c("coffee", "donut", "cookie"),
  c("tea", "donut")
)

coffee_trans <- as(coffee_data, "transactions")
```

6. Display a summary of `coffee_trans`. How dense is the matrix?

7. Create a bar chart of item frequencies. What items are tied in popularity?

8. Generate rules with `supp = 0.2` and `conf = 0.6`. How many rules result?

9. Use `subset()` to find rules with "coffee" as the LHS. What conclusions can you draw?

10. Find rules with "cookie" on the RHS and lift > 1.2. What does one of these rules suggest?

Dataset 3: Streaming Service Views

This dataset contains media genres watched together by streaming service users.

```
R Code
# Create streaming service transactions
streaming_data <- list(
  c("drama", "comedy"),
  c("comedy", "sci-fi"),
  c("documentary", "drama"),
  c("drama", "thriller"),
  c("sci-fi", "action"),
  c("drama", "comedy", "thriller"),
  c("action", "thriller"),
  c("documentary", "comedy"),
  c("drama", "sci-fi"),
  c("action", "documentary")
)

streaming_trans <- as(streaming_data,
                      "transactions")
```

11. View `inspect(streaming_trans)` and identify a genre pairing that appears more than once.

12. Generate association rules with support = 0.3 and confidence = 0.5. What genres commonly co-occur?

13. Subset rules where `lhs` includes "drama" and lift > 1. What are two key associations?

www.ingramcontent.com/pod-product-compliance
Lightning Source LLC
Chambersburg PA
CBHW051857210326
41597CB00033B/5931